TWENTY YEARS
OF ORGANISING IN THE
SHANTY TOWNS OF SOUTH AFRICA

TWENTY YEARS
OF COURAGE AND STRUGGLE

Abahlali baseMjondolo

Daraja Press

Published by
Daraja Press
https://darajapress.com
Wakefield, Quebec, Canada

© 2025 Abahlali baseMjondolo
ISBN: 978-1-997742-11-1

This book was produced through a collective process
organised by the movement that included two day-long meetings,
each with around forty participants, to generate the content,
followed by further meetings to review and edit the drafts.

Book design by Kate McDonnell

Catalogue in Publication data is available from
the Library and Archives of Canada

Freedom is a place we make. Abahlali raises socialism from the ground up. The movement's organizational energy combines practical necessity with political analysis that allows all members to participate. Abahlali is a model for change: while never rigid, it is firmly committed to ethical principles that enhance well-being by interrupting capitalist logic. This booklet shows the challenge, persistence, and beauty of emancipation in rehearsal. In other words, Abahlali is abolition in action.

> – **Ruth Wilson Gilmore**, Professor of Earth & Environmental Sciences and Director of the Center for Place, Culture, and Politics at the City University of New York Graduate Center

In the margins of South Africa's cities, where shackdwellers were told to disappear, Abahlali baseMjondolo has built something astonishing — communes that bloom in the cracks of empire, gardens named after the murdered, and a politics of dignity forged from the ground beneath their feet. For two decades, they have faced fire, flood, and assassinations with extraordinary courage, burying their dead while refusing to be erased, creating forms of life that insist another world is already here. Their story is not a metaphor but a map, offering movements everywhere fighting inequality and authoritarianism a blueprint for the stubborn, beautiful work of making freedom from below.

> — **Raj Patel**, award-winning author, film-maker and academic, Research Professor in the Lyndon B Johnson School of Public Affairs, University of Texas, Austin.

You have in your hands the remarkable story of the shack dwellers movement in South Africa (Abahlali baseMjondolo) covering the twenty years of its existence. It is a rich history of a grassroots democratic movement in its quest to humanize life in the present and to insist not only on the 'right to the city' but the right to collective occupy land and build such occupations collectively.

The history of Abahlali baseMjondolo is a story of sadness and betrayal since such resistance has not come without tremendous cost, violence and assassination. But what also shines through each page is the power of the movement's humanist philosophy, no one is illegal, everyone thinks and everyone must be counted and heard in a practice of solidarity and dialogue.

— **Nigel C. Gibson**, author of *Fanonian Practices in South Africa: From Steve Biko to Abahlali baseMjondolo* and editor of *Fanon Today: Reason and Revolt of the Wretched of the Earth*

Abahlali baseMjondolo:
Twenty years of courage and struggle

Today Abahlali baseMjondolo has more than 180,000 members in more than 100 branches in good standing across 4 provinces. It is the largest movement to have emerged in South Africa after apartheid and one of the largest movements of the urban poor anywhere in the world. The movement has won land and other victories for many thousands of people, built the democratic power of the oppressed from below, developed communities and won a powerful voice in public life. This has not been easy, and the movement has faced severe repression.

From its beginning, Abahlali baseMjondolo has not only been a movement to win and defend land, and then services and houses. It has also been a movement that has sought to live differently, to build new forms of life in the ruins of apartheid and the betrayals of the democratic state. It has built and run food gardens, crèches, community halls and kitchens, and political schools. It is a movement that works to build democracy and socialism from below. It is a movement that is deeply committed to political education and international solidarity.

Our members have always been expected to act with honesty, humility, accountability, and respect. Leaders are chosen by the people, remain answerable to them and can be recalled. The movement's insistence on dignity and principled conduct has been a compass through years marked by attempts at co-option and repression, including assassinations.

At their best occupations have become communes. The everyday work of survival and mutual support – the work of building communities – has been as important as the better-known battles against the state and the ruling party.

Spiritual and cultural life have been central to the movement's strength. Songs, prayers, and rituals have carried people through moments of grief and struggle, sustaining courage and unity. The work of building and sustaining resolve – inkani – and courage – isibindi – is always collective work.

These foundations – ethical discipline, the struggle for the necessities of everyday life, and a rich spiritual and cultural life – have sustained Abahlali through twenty years of repression, betrayal, and loss, and enabled the movement to continue to grow in strength, vision, and hope.

Today the movement works to build a movement of communes and a global movement of movements to affirm and defend the dignity of all people everywhere.

The History of Our Movement

In what is now South Africa, Dutch and then English colonialism began the process of making African people poor by violently seizing their land and cattle and destroying their political autonomy. Taxes were then imposed to force people into badly paid and highly exploitative forms of labour that kept some people poor while making others rich.

In 1948 a form of Afrikaner nationalism inspired by European fascism took control of the system of white supremacy. Five years later the African National Congress (ANC) and its allies began a process of collecting what it called 'freedom demands'. Its members travelled across the country asking people in rural villages, townships and factories to say in their own words what freedom should mean. Once these demands had been collected they were woven together into the Freedom Charter which was adopted at the Congress of the People in Kliptown in June 1955.

The Charter declared that "the land shall be shared among those who work it," calling for the abolition of racial restrictions on land ownership, the return of land to those dispossessed, and secure tenure for all. It also proclaimed that "all people shall have the right to live where they choose, be decently housed, and to bring up their families in comfort and security" and promised "houses, security and comfort". Taken together, these commitments recognised that genuine freedom required not only political rights but also the social and material foundations of dignity, affirming that equitable access to land and housing lay at the heart of a just society.

The ANC and other liberation movements were banned in 1960, after the Sharpeville massacre. After a period of retreat the formation of the Black Consciousness Movement in 1969 reinvigorated the political imagination. The formation of the black trade union movement after the Durban strikes in 1973, the Soweto uprising in 1976 and then the formation of the United Democratic Front (UDF) in Cape Town in 1983 brought millions of people into mass struggle.

Housing issues were often at the forefront of people's demands and the UDF and the trade union movement often found support in the growing urban land occupations and sometimes explicitly supported the right to occupy land. When the ANC was unbanned in 1990 there was a large banner in the foyer of its offices in Johannesburg that declared "Occupy the Cities!". The ANC spoke some of the language of the mass movements, but it moved fast to either bring them under control or to disband them.

In 1994 the ANC included land and housing in its electoral campaign and when the new Constitution was adopted in 1996 land and housing were recognised as fundamental rights. Section 25 affirmed that land reform is necessary to redress past dispossession, providing for equitable access to land and secure tenure for those previously denied it. Section 26 declared that "everyone has the right to have access to adequate housing" and obliged the state to take reasonable measures to achieve this right, while also protecting against arbitrary evictions. Together, these provisions placed a progressive duty on the state to ensure land justice and decent housing for all.

The ANC did begin a programme of building homes but the houses it built were much smaller and of much lower quality than the homes built for African people under apartheid. They were also often even further outside the cities than the townships built by apartheid. The government's housing programme swiftly became corrupt and a way for a few politically connected people to become absurdly wealthy. People who had occupied land during the mass struggles of the 1980s now found that they were being forcibly removed to wastelands far outside the cities. Many people were left homeless during these forced removals.

The rebellion of the poor comes to Durban

In 2004, ten years after the end of apartheid, people living in shack settlements in Johannesburg began to block roads with burning tyres – a form of protest common in urban settlements built on occupied land around the world. One of the first protests was organised in Diepsloot, a township in the northern edge of Johannesburg, on July 5, 2004, in response to rumours of a coming forced removal.

In August 2004 Tebogo Mkhonza, from Intabazwe township in Harrismith in the Free State, was shot dead by police during a protest. He was 17. In the years to come many more unarmed people would be killed by the police during these protests.

The media and groups with easy access to the media such as academics and NGOs depoliticised these protests by calling them 'service delivery protests'. This term implied that people just wanted government policies to be implemented more efficiently when in fact people were often protesting against those policies, and to demand the right to speak and decide for themselves on community matters. Others, though, referred to them as 'the rebellion of the poor'.

In Durban the long-established Kennedy Road settlement had a democratically elected leadership structure – the Kennedy Road Development Committee (KRDC). Its chairperson, S'bu Zikode, had arrived in Kennedy Road in 1997 after having to leave his university studies due to poverty. Conditions in the settlement were terrible. Shack fires were a common occurrence and there were only six public toilets for more than six thousand people. Worms accumulated at the back of the toilets. S'bu Zikode was deeply pained when he saw children eating the worms as they played behind the toilets.

The settlement had been democratised in 2000 with the formation of the KRDC, an elected structure which held weekly meetings, kept careful minutes, and organised various mutual aid community projects.

This was unlike most other settlements that were run by unelected people, such as in the nearby Foreman Road settlement where the domestic worker for the local ANC councillor ran the settlement.

S'bu Zikode had become active in the local ANC branch in 2000 and was elected as deputy chairperson of the ward in 2003. He carried mandates from shack dwellers into party meetings but quickly found that these were dismissed. The meetings were dominated by middle-class members who treated shack settlements as an embarrassment or a problem to be managed, rather than communities to be engaged with on equal terms. "We were expected to be voting cattle," S'bu later recalled, "but when it came to decisions, our voices meant nothing."

A decisive break came in 2004. Housing officials convened a meeting to discuss a long-promised housing development for Kennedy Road but excluded the settlement and even its ANC branch from the discussion. Residents later discovered that rather than houses being built on the land that had been promised to them it had been sold to a local businessman to build brick factory. Plans had been made to 'relocate' the residents of Kennedy Road far outside the city. Such 'relocations' – which the movement later called 'forced removals' – always left many people homeless.

In late 2004, S'bu Zikode resigned from the ANC and the KRDC declared that 2005 would be a "Year of Action." On 16 February a KRDC-convened mass meeting at Kennedy Road resolved to demand an immediate response on land and housing and, if ignored, to organise a road blockade. The resolution was minuted and adopted as a collective mandate, setting the "Year of Action" in motion.

On 19 March 2005, the growing national wave of protest arrived in Durban when about 750 Kennedy Road residents blockaded the M19, which connects to the N2, with burning tyres and logs for around four hours. They demanded to be able to speak to their ANC ward councillor, Yacoob Baig. When he arrived in an armoured police vehicle, he told the police the protesters were criminals and should be arrested. The police moved in with dogs and teargas and arrested fourteen people, including two schoolchildren. Many other people were beaten.

The day after the Kennedy Road blockade, residents gathered in the settlement to plan their response to the fourteen arrests. They agreed that contributions would be collected toward bail and began to prepare for a march on the police station the following day.

On the following day, 21 March 2005, which was Human Rights Day, about 1,200 residents marched to the Sydenham police station demanding the release of the detainees under the slogan "release them or arrest us all." They were attacked by the police and beaten back into the settlement by large numbers of police with highly militarised equipment including armoured vehicles. Richard Pithouse, a young academic, arrived at the settlement during a tense stand-off between a large group of young men and the police at the entrance to the settlement.

The residents had decided that the accused would represent themselves in court, but they were not given a chance to speak, and bail was denied. The fourteen detainees, including the two children, spent ten days in custody before being released after legal support was accessed. Their bail of R10,000 was raised collectively, with each household asked to contribute R10. When the fourteen returned home, a welcome celebration was held in the Kennedy Road community hall.

In the weeks that followed, the KRDC, which included people like Nhlanhla Mzobe, Zandile Nsibande, and others, convened daily meetings. Richard Pithouse, who was now working with the KRDC and participating in its weekly meetings, introduced two other academics, Fazel Khan and Raj Patel, to the KRDC and they also began working with the KRDC.

The struggle expands beyond Kennedy Road

S'bu Zikode was invited to visit nearby shack settlements, including Foreman Road, Jadhu Place, Quarry Road, and Pemary Ridge, to report on events and discuss shared concerns. Foreman Road became an early and strong supporter of the process that led up to the formation of the movement, with Mqapheli Bonono, Mnikelo

Ndabankulu and Lungisani Jama being among the key participants in the political work there. When S'bu Zikode and Richard
Pithouse were first invited to visit the settlement Mqapheli Bonono
and others had to provide security in a very tense atmosphere as
the ANC attempted to prevent the meeting from going ahead.

Residents from these nearby settlements began to attend
meetings at Kennedy Road, building a wider process of cooper-
ation. In the two weeks before the September march, there were
nightly meetings across nearby settlements, often preceded by
screenings of the film Kennedy Road and the Councillor, which
had been made by Fazel Khan and a friend of his, Sally Gilles,
and followed by collective discussion. In Foreman Road there
was still tense struggle against the ANC to create the space for
independent discussion and organisation and a line of young
people had to hold the space for the film to be shown.

A clear set of demands emerged from these processes. People
wanted to be able to organise themselves freely, speak for themselves and participate in all decision making relating to their communities. They also opposed forced removals to what were called
the 'human dumping grounds' on the urban periphery and for
land and housing to be provided in the cities. The government
was insisting that shack settlements would be eradicated – first
by 2010 and then by 2014 – and saying that because shack settlements were temporary basic services such as water, sanitation,
electricity, drainage, paths and fire protection would not be provided. People also insisted that these services must be provided.

On 13 May 2005, more than 3,000 people marched on
Yacoob Baig, demanding land, housing, and his resignation. This
was a legal protest and the first major protest after the blockade,
and it drew in support from neighbouring settlements. From this
moment on the ANC, and some other forces from among the
elite, insisted that the struggles emerging from the shack settlements in Clare Estate and surrounding areas were driven by a
white man working for a foreign government to destabilise the

ANC. They called this the 'Third Force'. It was clear that they could not understand that poor African people could think and speak for themselves. At this point the movement had no funding other than what its own members could provide.

On 14 September 2005, over 5,000 residents marched again on Yacoob Baig, demanding toilets, land, and an end to threats of forced removal. The protestors carried a coffin and staged a mock funeral for the councillor. They said that "if Baig does not resign we, ourselves, will declare that Ward 25 does not have a councillor and govern ourselves."

On 4 October 2005, more than 1,000 residents of the Quarry Road shack settlement marched on Councillor Jayraj Bachu, demanding the return of toilets that had been removed and land and housing in the city. The march was organised by the Quarry Road Development Committee with support from other settlements. Protesters staged another mock funeral. This action followed earlier repression at Quarry Road, including a violent police response to a protest against the removal of toilets in December 2004. At the time of the October march, a 17-year-old from the settlement was still in prison awaiting trial.

Later that same day, leaders from fourteen shack settlements met at Kennedy Road. There were 32 elected representatives present – 17 men and 15 women. They agreed to form one organisation to unite their struggles. They named it Abahlali baseMjondolo. The aim of the new movement was to struggle from below for a new society to be born where everyone is seen and respected as a person – a society where there is equality – ukulingana – and justice – ubulungiswa.

The new movement is repressed

On 21 October, a fire destroyed sixteen shacks in Kennedy Road. One-year-old Mhlengi Khumalo was badly burned and died on 22 October, at King Edward Hospital. A memorial service was held on 28 October, in the Kennedy Road community hall. The statement issued in advance of the memorial to mourn the child, noted that "Ugesi, umhlaba, nezindlu ngabe kuyiphephisile impilo yakhe" ("Electricity, land and housing would have made his life safer") and linked the tragedy to the City's withdrawal of basic services from shack settlements.

On 9 November S'bu Zikode published an article in the *Daily News* titled 'We are the Third Force.' It answered claims that Abahlali was manipulated by a hidden 'third force'. S'bu Zikode explained that poor black people think and act for themselves, and that the real 'third force driving the movement was the lived experience of poverty and exclusion. It caused a sensation and was widely republished and translated, becoming a foundational moment in the shaping the movement's public voice.

Abahlali decided to march directly on the City's highest authority, Mayor Obed Mlaba, on 14 November 2005. The march was organised from the Foreman Road settlement, with support from the other nearby settlements where people had joined the movement. The memorandum, developed through a process of careful discussion, called for land within the city to be made available for housing, the provision of basic services such as water, electricity, sanitation, and refuse collection, and an immediate end to forced removals to peripheral 'human dumping grounds' It also demanded that the municipality engage directly with shack dwellers in decisions affecting their lives, rather than treating them as a nuisance to be spoken for by councillors or officials. Above all, it insisted that shack dwellers be recognised as equal citizens with the right to live in the city in dignity.

The march was set for 14 November 2005. Abahlali applied for permission under the Regulation of Gatherings Act and gave proper notice. In response, Mike Sutcliffe, the City Manager of eThekwini, issued a formal but unlawful instruction that the march would not be permitted. Abahlali challenged the ban in court and won the legal right to march. Sutcliffe and the municipality ignored the judgment.

On the morning of 14 November, thousands of shack dwellers gathered at Foreman Road. Armoured vehicles and riot police with shields, batons, and teargas were positioned to block the entrance to the road outside the settlement. Lungisani Jama, a respected leader in Foreman Road, asked the gathered people how they wanted to proceed. There was a discussion and a clear consensus that people wanted to march in defiance of the ban. When the marchers attempted to move out of the shack settlement and onto the road the police attacked and made arrests. A police officer fired live ammunition from his pistol. Several people were injured, and the planned march to City Hall was stopped before it could leave Foreman Road. The police attack on the march was the lead story on the television news that night and reported internationally – in the *New York Times, The Economist, Al Jazeera* etc. This was the first time that the movement began to be known elsewhere in the world. Lungisani Jama passed away in July 2007. Mqapheli Bonono remembers that "he laid a clear road forward for the movement for and from Foreman Road."

From 14 November onwards all requests by Abahlali to march were unlawfully refused by Mike Sutcliffe until 27 February the following year when a court order was secured interdicting Sutcliffe and the police from interfering with Abahlali's right to march.

In the months following the Kennedy Road blockade and the founding of the movement activists in settlements affiliated to the movement came under daily police harassment. This escalated after the March on Mlaba and Foreman Road was hit particularly hard. Police regularly entered settlements at night, shining torches into shacks, forcing their way inside, and sometimes breaking down doors. People were insulted, questioned, and threatened. Beatings and arbitrary arrests were common. Mqapheli Bonono was among those singled out for repeated harassment. The three academics who had been supporting the movement – Fazel Khan, Raj Patel and Richard Pithouse – all faced combined pressure from the municipality and a network of left academics who thought that they should be controlling social movements and were all forced out of their jobs.

A small network of left academics that had been linked to the first wave of post-apartheid social movements had often exercised significant influence over those movements via donor funding. In Durban, where Patrick Bond and Ashwin Desai were the leading figures, there was openly hostility to the development of democratic, member-led structures. As those early formations began to fall apart, some – but not all – of the academics involved treated Abahlali baseMjondolo's insistence on taking direction from its members with immediate hostility. They assumed for themselves an unelected, unmandated right to give direction to movements.

Not long after the movement's formation Desai, who had previously led resistance to evictions from municipal flats in Chatsworth, ran a meeting with support from the Centre for Civil Society at the university at which three middle class people – none of whom was African – claimed to represent four movements, all of which only existed on paper. It was said that Abahlali baseMjondolo should join with these four other 'movements' to form one big movement in which each movement would have the same weight. The movement declined to accept this kicking off even more intense hostility. There would be years of slander from this quarter.

Local elections were coming and Abahlali baseMjondolo were invited to participate in a live recording of the SABC's Asikhulume talk show at the Cato Crest Hall on 12 February 2006. They were invited to bring sixty members and told that seats would be reserved for them. However, at the doors, police blocked anyone in a red shirt from entering the hall. When S'bu Zikode presented the written invitation, a police officer assaulted him. Abahlali regrouped outside and pressed forward, banging on the glass doors at the back of the hall. In the ensuing confusion S'bu Zikode and Philani Zungu entered the hall. Immediately after S'bu Zikode began speaking, the power was cut and the broadcast collapsed.

On 27 February, the Durban High Court granted Abahlali baseMjondolo an urgent interdict after City Manager Mike Sutcliffe had unlawfully banned a planned march into the city. The order confirmed that the march was and remained legal, interdicted both Sutcliffe and the police from interfering, and imposed punitive costs on the municipality. This brought an end to Sutcliffe's attempt to ban the movement's marches.

The movement adopted a "No Land! No House! No Vote!" boycott position ahead of the 1 March municipal elections. This developed the Landless People's Movement's (LPM) "No Land, No Vote" call first made in 2004, which met serious hostility and repression, including arrests and torture. It was a tactical refusal to vote for the ANC while shack-dwellers were denied well-located land, decent housing, and basic services, and faced repression when they organised. As with the LPM's 2004 position it was met with intense hostility from a range of elites some of whom said that the movement needed 'political education'.

On 21 April 2006, the KwaZulu-Natal government publicly announced the Slums Bill. The Bill repeated the logic of earlier colonial legislation that criminalised the self-organised occupation of urban land and self-built housing and sought to compel the state and private property owners to evict. The movement began a process of collective discussion around the Bill via line-by-line readings.

On 27 April 2006, the movement hosted its first UnFreedom Day in Durban "to mourn the denial of our collective rights" and declare that there is "no freedom for the poor." It was a modest event held in a hall in Sydenham.

On 1 September 2006, at meetings in the offices of Kwa-Zulu-Natal Housing MEC Mike Mabuyakhulu, officials warned Abahlali's leaders not to speak to the media and told them they should join Slum Dwellers International (SDI) if they wanted regular engagement. This followed a meeting in July at which Abahlali leaders were accused of being "agents of a foreign government" and instructed to affiliate to SDI. SDI is a top down international liberal NGO network. Abahlali refused to affiliate, insisting on movement autonomy.

On 12 September 2006, S'bu Zikode and Philani Zungu were stopped by Sydenham police on their way to a radio debate with the MEC. They were arrested on spurious charges and assaulted in custody. Station commander Glen Nayager beat them, at one point sneering, "Do you think you're the Jesus Christ of the jondolos?" Philani's head was smashed against a wall, and he was knocked unconscious. News of the arrests spread quickly. People rushed to the Sydenham Police Station from Kennedy Road, Foreman Road and other settlements. That evening an emergency mass meeting at Kennedy Road was attacked by police with rubber bullets and teargas. Nondumiso Mke was shot in the knee with live ammunition.

S'bu later described a sleepless night in the holding cells of the Sydenham Police Station – badly bruised, in pain, and wrestling with whether he should continue – saying the beating was meant to make him feel "weightless." On 13 September, when he and Philani appeared in the Durban Magistrates' Court, the corridors were filled with people in red shirts from across the affiliated settlements. Seeing them settled it: he would continue and commit his life to the struggle.

After prolonged litigation, on 22 April 2013 the Durban High Court ordered the Minister of Police to pay a total of R195,000 in damages to S'bu, Philani and Nondumiso.

In late 2005 Abahlali baseMjondolo had attended the Social Movements Indaba in Johannesburg, an NGOs and academic run project to connect grassroots organisations in which the NGO and academic people set the agenda and ran the meeting. Abahlali and other grassroots formations, most notably the Western Cape Anti-Eviction Campaign but including the Landless Peoples' Movement, challenged this and secured agreement that the next gathering would be hosted by the movements in Durban.

The movements worked together to plan the meeting, set for December 2006, and to be hosted by Centre for Civil Society. Shortly before it began, the NGOs circulated an agenda imposed without consultation. The first response of the movements was not to attend. But, after a meeting at Kennedy Road with activists from the Western Cape Anti-Eviction Campaign and the Landless Peoples' Movement, the decision was taken to protest at the SMI meeting at the university The academics hosting the event responded by calling security, and NGO bosses and academics publicly labelled Abahlali as "criminals" and falsely claimed a white man had orchestrated the protest – a claim rooted in the same assumption long shared by ANC officials that poor Black people cannot think and act for themselves. No white person had participated in the discussion that led to the decision to protest.

From 2007 the new Motala Heights branch in Pinetown faced sustained intimidation from Ricky Govender, a notorious local gangster and 'businessman' who was trying to evict poor people – Indian and African – to expropriate the land they were living on and build private housing. This marked the movement's first prolonged confrontation with a private criminal network. The struggle was led by two brave women – Shamitha Naidoo and Louisa Motha. On 5 August 2007 Govender assaulted Naidoo and threatened to have her killed. On 12 June 2008, the Durban High Court granted interdicts against Govender, several associates, the Pinetown SAPS station commander and the Minister of Safety & Security. Intimidation and evictions continued – including an eviction of 23 families on 6 August 2009, and the bulldozing of a Shembe temple on 16 January 2011 – but in the end Govender's' power was broken, and the evictions stopped.

At 3 a.m. on 21 March 2007, police arrested members of the KRDC on bogus charges. Nine people were initially detained, including eight KRDC members. After a sit-in at the Sydenham police station four women were released, leaving six residents in custody. They became known as the "Kennedy 6". Bail was refused and they were transferred to Westville Prison. On 3 April 2007, five of the detainees began a hunger strike to press for bail and protest against their detention. After sustained public mobilisation and legal action the court granted bail on 24 May 2007 and the six were released. The case then dragged on into 2008, when the charges were finally withdrawn.

On 21 June 2007, the KwaZulu-Natal Legislature passed the Elimination and Prevention of Re-emergence of Slums Act despite detailed representations from community organisations, lawyers and academics. Abahlali delegates attended the sitting in June and were denied the right to speak. The movement resolved to oppose the law politically and to prepare a legal challenge. Stuart Wilson, who co-founded the Socio-Economic Rights Institute (SERI) agreed to take the case.

On 10 April 2007, activists held a candlelit protest outside Sydenham Police Station against assaults, arbitrary arrests and intimidation, directing their memorandum to Station Commander Glen Nayager. The statement declared that Nayager was treating shack dwellers as criminals – "you have decided to make the poor your enemy" – and called for an end to police brutality and the criminalisation of the movement.

On 27 April 2007, Abahlali held its second UnFreedom Day in the Kennedy Road settlement in defiance of an unlawful ban by the municipality. This was a much bigger event, which continued while a police helicopter circled low above the meeting.

On 28 September around 3,000 people proceeded peacefully to Yacoob Baig's office to deliver a memorandum to Obed Mlaba. Permission had been given for the march on the mayor, but it was attacked with batons and a water cannon without warning to disperse been given. Numerous people, including clergy, suffered minor injuries and six people were seriously injured and required hospitalisation. Mam Kikine, an elderly woman, was shot five times in the back at close range with rubber bullets. Thirteen people were arrested on the charges of 'Violating the Gatherings

Act' and 'Public Violence'. When Mnikelo Ndabankulu arrived at the station to check on his comrades he was also arrested.

On 26 January 2008, Nkosingiphile Cwera, a four-month-old infant, died after a rat bite in the family's shack in Kennedy Road. A memorial was held at the settlement on 2 February 2008. Abahlali reminded the wider public that the City had long been warned about the rat problem. As S'bu Zikode put it, "rubbish is not removed, which provides a breeding ground for these rodents."

A person is a person wherever they find themselves

In May 2008, xenophobic violence began in Johannesburg and spread across the country, leaving at least 62 people dead and more than 100,000 displaced. After careful collective discussion on two consecutive days, Abahlali baseMjondolo issued a public statement on 21 May 2008 that circulated globally and was widely translated.

The movement affirmed that Unyawo alunampumulo – that "a person is a person wherever they find themselves." It stated: "There is only one human race. An action can be illegal. A person cannot be illegal." The statement committed Abahlali to work with street traders, migrant organisations and others on practical support, and to "shelter and defend" people under attack. Today opposition to xenophobia remains one of the movement's central principles.

Years later, reflecting on this moment, Zikode said the movement had long spoken about dignity for its members, but in 2008 it had to affirm that it was committed to dignity for everyone.

The Youth League was formed on 16 June with Bongo Dlamini taking a leading role. Many of the people who had taken a leading role in building the movement – such as S'bu Zikode, Mnikelo Ndabankulu and Mqapheli Bonono – were young at the time, and the movement has always had young people in leadership. However, the formation of the Youth League created a space to specifically develop young people into leaders.

The Women's League was formed on 9 August and Zandile Nsibande was elected as its first leader. From the beginning, women have made up about 60% of the movement's members and women have been central to the life of the movement. They have organised and led occupations and branches, and sustained communities through the everyday work of survival. The establishment of a Women's League created a space where women could organise together and build confidence.

In the same month the movement held its first public event in Cape Town. The attempts to expand the movement into Cape Town did not succeed. Part of the problem was the physical distance from Durban and there was also the usual problem of NGO capture. Another problem was that some of the people that joined had been leaders in now defunct organisations and brought the forms of politics that they had learnt in those organisations into the attempt to build the movement in Cape Town.

This was also the year in which residents of eMacambini in northern KwaZulu-Natal approached Abahlali for support when Ruwaad Holdings, a Dubai-based company, announced plans for a massive 'AmaZulu World' theme park development. The project threatened to displace as many as 50,000 people – around 10,000 families – along with schools, clinics and ancestral graves. With Abahlali's backing, about 5,000 residents organised mass resistance, blockading the N2 and R102 on 4 December 2008. The resistance was effective: the plan was eventually abandoned.

In January 2009 the movement began to resist attempts to remove families in the Siyanda settlement to the Richmond Farm Transit Camp. 'Transit camps' – essentially government-built and managed shacks – forced people into terrible living conditions while creating opportunities for the ANC to take political control over communities and for profiting from the construction and maintenance of the camps.

A court hearing on 30 January 2009 was adjourned to 6 March, but despite legal resistance, families were forcibly moved to the camp in March 2009, catalysing a sustained movement-wide opposition to transit camps as indefinite, unsafe "temporary" warehousing that violate human dignity. In September 2012, the High Court ordered the municipality to provide permanent housing to affected Richmond Farm households.

The Attack on the Movement in Kennedy Road

Beginning with Jacob Zuma's 2006 rape trial and continuing through his 2007 campaign for the ANC presidency and his 2009 national election campaign, Zulu nationalism took hold in KwaZulu-Natal. Abahlali baseMjondolo had always been a multi-ethnic movement and did not join the support for Zuma. As the political climate intensified, the movement came under increasing pressure and there was a general sense of threat. This escalated in mid-November when John Mchunu, the chairperson of the eThekwini Region of the ANC said "The element of these NGO who are funded by the West to destabilise us; these elements use all forms of media and poor people. We know them very well; we have seen them using their power at Abahlali baseMjondolo."

On the night of 26 September 2009, a youth meeting was underway in the Kennedy Road community hall when about forty men, heavily armed with pangas and large knives, entered the settlement identifying themselves as amaZulu and as ANC. They first attacked the meeting and then went house-to-house, targeting people who were prominent in the movement and amaMpondo residents. Homes were ransacked and destroyed, and some were burnt. Despite repeated urgent requests, the police did not intervene during the attack.

People began to spontaneously resist, and an ethnically marked conflict developed. Two people – Mthokozisi Thabani Ndlovu and Ndumiso Thokozani Mnguni – were killed. Hundreds, by some counts more than a thousand, were immediately displaced as families fled in fear. When the attackers reached

Zikode's home and found it empty, they destroyed and burned the house and looted its contents. Filmmakers working on what became the award-winning film *Dear Mandela* recorded aspects of the turmoil that night.

The next day thirteen people were arrested, denied bail and detained in Westville Prison. They were all isiXhosa speakers. KwaZulu-Natal MEC for Safety & Security Willies Mchunu arrived, presented the movement as criminal, condemned it for taking the provincial government to court to oppose the Slums Act and announced that it has been 'disbanded'. After one case was withdrawn the remaining accused – known as the "Kennedy 12" were kept in prison.

At the time of the attack S'bu Zikode was away in Estcourt. He returned the next day and, following direct threats to his life and to other leaders, went underground. The first clandestine meeting after the attack was held in a funeral parlour. Later, meetings cautiously moved into public spaces as reorganisation continued under threat.

Over the following months, particularly on weekends, the homes of Abahlali members and supporters were systematically destroyed, and many were driven from the settlement. Again, the police refused to intervene. Some members left Durban for the Eastern Cape and did not return.

Prior to the attack Zikode had been asked to keep a large sum of money safe – around R300,000 – by a street traders' stokvel. The box in which the money was kept was secured and it was returned to the stokvel. Word that the money had been returned when it could so easily have been said to have been stolen quickly spread and the movement's standing among poor people in Durban was elevated.

However, in the immediate period after the attack the movement was seriously isolated on the middle-class terrain. The same academic and NGO figures that had been hostile to the movement from the outset enthusiastically backed the ANC/state/police propaganda, and this was very damaging. Abahlali consistently called for a judicial inquiry into the attack, its organisation, and the conduct of officials and police before and during the violence. Bishop Rubin Phillip was the only South African public figure who openly stood with the movement at this time and the Socio-Economic Rights Institute (SERI) and the Church Land Programme (CLP) were the only NGOs to stand with the movement.

However, internationally, prominent scholars – including Noam Chomsky – expressed support. After seeing the statement signed by Chomsky, the U.S. Consulate made contact, and Zikode was invited to travel to Washington to meet President Barack Obama at the White House on a special visa arranged via the International Visitor Leadership Program. The movement was very surprised to receive this invitation but after careful discussion it was, for tactical reasons, decided to accept the invitation, as it was thought that it was likely to reduce the risks of further repression at a time when Zikode and others were under open death threats and the movement's survival was in doubt.

As testimonies, good journalism, and academic research accumulated, the truth became clearer to good faith observers. In July the case against the Kennedy 12 was thrown out before the defence was even called. After the prosecution closed its case, the magistrate dismissed the charges, describing key state witnesses as "unreliable," "dishonest," and "belligerent." Both the ANC and the academics and NGO figures that had supported their propaganda lost their credibility. Speaking off the record senior figures in the ANC later said that John Mchunu had ordered the attack.

September 2009 marked a new phase in the life of the movement. From 2005 to 2009, repression had largely come via the police, and much of the movement's work focused on defending existing shack settlements against eviction. After 2009, repression was increasingly subcontracted to armed party thugs, and Abahlali shifted towards occupying new land – a change that came to define the next phase of the movement's life.

Victory in the Constitutional Court

On 14 October, while the movement was still reeling from the attack, the Constitutional Court handed down judgment in Abahlali baseMjondolo Movement SA and Another v Premier of KwaZulu-Natal and Others upholding the appeal and declaring section 16 of the KwaZulu-Natal Slums Act unconstitutional and invalid for conflicting with the constitutional and legislative requirements for just and equitable evictions. There was a sense of tremendous joy in the court, and in the movement – joy that poor people had been able to successfully use the law to confront the government and joy that the movement had won such an important victory in such a difficult time. Minutes after the judgment, an academic working with Abahlali received a telephonic death threat. The ruling ended the state's fantasy that shacks would be eradicated by administrative fiat and opened the way for in-situ upgrading and the provision of services, with any evictions subject to strict constitutional safeguards.

After the victory in the Constitutional Court there was some respite from repression, which continued through 2010, the year of the football World Cup. That respite was short lived. On 13 October 2011, Abahlali met eThekwini Mayor James Nxumalo for the first time. At the meeting, Nigel Gumede – Chair of the Housing Portfolio Committee – introduced himself as "a murderer," declared that the ANC was at war with Abahlali, and threatened to ambush S'bu Zikode in the forest. Gumede had made openly ethnic remarks about the movement after the 2009 attack.

On 5 November 2011, the movement responded to these open threats by marching from Botha Park to the City Hall to demand Gumede's removal as Housing Portfolio Chair, citing years of threats, illegal evictions, armed disconnections, forced removals to rural dumping grounds, transit camps, corruption, violations of court orders, and defective houses, while residents continued to face shack fires and life-threatening conditions.

In 2012 the courts became an increasingly important terrain of struggle. As the movement said at the time, "Courts are not our home, but they can be a weapon." On 27 January, the Durban High Court set aside an eviction in Shallcross. On 19 September, the court ordered permanent housing within three months for 37 Siyanda families who had been warehoused at the Richmond Farm Transit Camp. On 25 September, the movement filed a damages claim over the 2009 Kennedy Road attack. And on 7 December a march from the Palmiet Road settlement went ahead after an attempt by the police to prohibit the march was overturned in court. A memorandum was delivered to Premier Zweli Mkhize and Ward 23 Councillor Themba Mtshali.

In 2013 the municipality began openly defying court orders, demolishing shacks and evicting people in contempt of interdicts. It then sought to give this a veneer of legality by seeking and winning in interim blanket interdict on 28 March. This order authorized the municipality and police to prevent land occupations, remove materials, and demolish unauthorized structures on specific properties. At the same time there was a clear turn to open repression, felt most intensely in Cato Crest.

The assassinations begin

On 15 March, community leader Thembinkosi Qumbelo was assassinated. He was not an Abahlali member, but was a well-known housing activist in Cato Crest. His killing was linked locally to the new land occupation in the area, which residents named Marikana after the mineworkers' strike the previous year. The occupation was organised in response to a corrupt housing project in which houses were being allocated to ANC members.

On 26 June, Abahlali local leader Nkululeko Gwala was murdered. Days earlier he had raised questions about corruption in the allocation of houses. That night the ANC called a public meeting in Cato Crest, chaired by Mayor James Nxumalo and Sibongiseni Dhlomo, then the regional chairperson of the

ANC. From the platform Gwala was described as a troublemaker who should be "removed", with Dhlomo telling the mayor to "take him home" to Inchanga, his home village. Later that night Gwala was ambushed and shot twelve times while walking home.

Gwala's funeral was held in Inchanga on 3 July 2013. The atmosphere was extremely tense. The ANC sought to turn the occasion into an ANC funeral, asserting authority over the family and community. The local councillor spoke first, emphasising that Inchanga was an ANC stronghold and attempting to frame the service as an ANC event. He mocked the presence of shack dwellers, saying there were no shacks in Inchanga but that "people from the shacks" were there, a remark aimed directly at Abahlali.

High-level figures, including Mayor James Nxumalo, were present alongside large numbers of police and intelligence officers. Abahlali leaders recognised the threat and counselled S'bu Zikode not to speak, fearing it was too dangerous. But when the master of ceremonies, appointed by the family, called him, he decided he could not remain silent.

Zikode spoke directly against the narrative set by the ANC councillor. He said the family deserved the truth, and explained that Gwala was killed for his honesty and bravery, for refusing corruption, and because he stood with the oppressed. He reminded mourners that senior ANC politicians had publicly threatened Gwala on the very day of his assassination. He told the gathering: "He died for the homeless people of Durban, the province and the whole country. He died for the people who are angry because the leaders don't want to listen to them. The leaders are killing us because they see us as a hindrance to their abuse of tenders."

The response was electric. The crowd moaned in grief, the marquee shook, and even the police and intelligence officers stood up in agitation. Comrades quickly pulled Zikode out of the marquee for his safety, as the tension was severe. ANC leaders were unable to continue with their programme. The local councillor slipped away, and the mayor remained silent. From that moment, the funeral shifted. What the ANC had sought to control became, in the end, an Abahlali funeral.

The speech was carried live on uKhozi FM and appeared on the front page of *Isolezwe*. It had reached a wide audience across Durban and became a major political event in the city.

On 21 September, during an illegal eviction at the Marikana occupation, Abahlali member Nkosinathi Mngomezulu was shot several times with live ammunition by the Land Invasion Unit. He lingered in hospital for some time, but never recovered, and later died after a long and painful decline caused by his injuries.

On 26 September, Abahlali organised coordinated road blockades in protest at repression in Cato Crest. Four days later, on 30 September, Nqobile Nzuza (17) was shot in the back of the head and killed by police during a blockade. Police claimed they had come under attack and fired in defence of their lives, and this was widely reported as fact. In reality, Nzuza had been shot while running away. In 2018 Constable Phumlani Ndlovu was convicted of her murder and sentenced to ten years in prison.

On the same day that Nzuza was killed, Abahlali's General Secretary Bandile Mdlalose was arrested while visiting the family. She was later released on bail under restrictive conditions, including being barred from entering Cato Manor.

By the end of 2013, repression in Cato Crest included the murders of Qumbelo and Gwala, the shooting and later death of Mngomezulu, the killing of Nzuza by police, repeated demolitions in defiance of court orders, and the arrest of leaders. Local ANC structures, the municipality and the police had acted together in a systematic campaign of repression.

Confronting corruption

In 2014 the movement faced its first corruption issue resulting in the expulsion of Bandile Mdlalose, who was serving as Secretary-General. She had been approached by people in a block of flats seeking support against a threatened eviction. She did not inform the movement of this and told the occupiers that she could arrange lawyers for them. She collected "membership fees" from them at an inflated rate of R50 rather than the standard R20 and took more money from them claiming that she needed to travel to Johannesburg to meet with lawyers from SERI. No such meetings took place and SERI was never briefed on the matter. When the court date came Mdlalose was not there and there were no lawyers. The residents were evicted.

The residents brought a formal complaint to Abahlali. A disciplinary hearing was convened on 6 April 2014, which she refused to attend. After carefully considering the evidence, the movement expelled her.

Mdlalose was swiftly given a job at the Centre for Civil Society (CCS) at the University of KwaZulu-Natal. At the same time she joined Black First Land First, a very small organisation producing propaganda for Jacob Zuma and the Gupta brothers, and threatening their critics. Shortly after joining CCS defamatory messages were sent from her email address to a large number of academics, NGOs, and journalists around the world. These messages repeated, almost word for word, the same accusations, personal hatreds and turns of phrase that Heinrich Böhmke – who was linked to Ashwin Desai and Patrick Bond and now associated with CCS – had used against the movement from the moment it became clear that it would not accept the authority of the dominant faction of the middle class left in Durban.

A fraudulent and defamatory article was published in Bandile's name in the academic journal *Politikon*. Abahlali sought the right to a full and fair reply but were refused. Despite further requests for a right to reply made to the journal's editor and board – as late as 2025 – this right has never been granted. The article remains on record without Abahlali being given a right of reply.

On 7 May 2014 Abahlali took a tactical decision that, while it proved to be effective, shocked some of the movement's supporters. On 7 May, at an open mass meeting, the movement voted

– not by consensus but through a show of hands – to call on its members to cast their ballots for the Democratic Alliance (DA) in the coming national election. The proposal was put forward by Mnikelo Ndabankulu and debated before being carried.

The movement stressed that this was not an endorsement of the DA, whose politics remained fundamentally at odds with its own, but a tactical move aimed at punishing the ANC for its role in assassinations, illegal evictions, and the killing of young people by the police. There was not an immediate halt to repression but years later, the political analyst Imraan Buccus, noting that there were no assassinations of Abahlali leaders in 2015 or 2016, wrote that "impeccable sources in the ANC" had told him that this decision prompted an instruction to be delivered to local ANC structures to halt the repression.

On 29 September 2014 Thuli Ndlovu, chairperson of the KwaNdengezi branch, was assassinated inside her home. Gunmen entered while she was helping a child with homework. She was shot dead in front of her children, and another person in the house was also shot and wounded. Thuli had been outspoken against corruption in the allocation of houses in KwaNdengezi and had openly challenged ANC councillors. In 2016 two ANC councillors, Mduduzi Ngcobo and Velile Lutsheku, together with a hitman, were convicted of her murder and sentenced to life imprisonment.

First connections with the MST

In 2015 Abahlali began building direct ties with Brazil's Movimento dos Trabalhadores Rurais Sem Terra (MST). Until then, connections with global movements had been largely monopolised by NGOs and academics, some of whom were hostile to Abahlali and to any grassroots struggles that insisted on respect for their autonomy. MST had deliberately bypassed these intermediaries and sent a cadre, Augusto Juncal, to South Africa to establish direct contact. This opened the way for sustained movement-to-movement solidarity grounded in reciprocity rather than NGO mediation.

The new relationship quickly bore fruit. In 2015 Thina Kha-nyile became the first Abahlali comrade to attend the MST's Escola Nacional Florestan Fernandes (ENFF) near São Paulo. At the same time Richard Pithouse was teaching there, and Juncal had already given Abahlali cadres preliminary training in South Africa to prepare them for the experience. Khanyile's attendance marked the beginning of a steady flow of militants to the ENFF. Later, Abahlali members would return not just as students but also as teachers, sharing their own experiences with comrades from across the world.

The following year, 2016, began with the horrific murder of Isaac Mabika, a branch coordinator, who was killed in an axe attack at his home in Briardene on 6 February. By May 2016, amid escalating repression, the movement had begun to speak of a 'gangster state.' From this point onward it increasingly argued that assassination, threats and corruption were driven by the intersection of criminality and politics.

While the meeting was still reeling from the horrific murder of Isaac Mabika the relationship with the MST deepened as Mqapheli Bonono participated in a class at the ENFF for the first time. His experience there was formative, and he would go on to lead the relationship with the MST, which became one of the most important international connections in Abahlali's history. As Mqapheli Bonono later remembered, what struck Abahlali most was the respect with which they were treated at the school: "we were taken serious." That contrasted sharply with many South African NGO workshops, where poor people were often patronised and manipulated.

Mqapheli Bonono later returned to Brazil as a teacher, sharing Abahlali's experience of land occupations and grassroots democracy with militants from across the world. He recalls that the MST emphasised that land could not be sold or commodified within the movement, and that occupations had to be defended and organised collectively. These principles resonated deeply with Abahlali's own experience. Over time the MST's practices of building cooperatives, organising production, and creating communal spaces would shape how Abahlali began to think about turning occupations into communes.

On 20 August 2016, the Durban High Court set aside the interim interdict that the municipality had obtained in March 2013, and had used for more than two years to justify shack demolitions across the city. This outcome was the result of a determined legal challenge by Abahlali, with the support of SERI. From the day the order was granted, Abahlali had argued that it was unlawful, and their persistence eventually forced the matter back before the court. The victory vindicated what the movement had said all along – that the municipality had been demolishing people's homes illegally. But it came after thousands had already lost their homes under the cover of the unlawful order.

On 15 October 2016 the Good Hope branch was launched in Germiston, Gauteng. The branch did not succeed due to challenges with the leadership, but it became the base for two new land occupations. The first was crushed but the second – the Lindokuhle Mnguni land occupation – is now a successful commune.

On 5 November, S'bu Zikode travelled to the Third World Meeting of Popular Movements in the Vatican. In addition to addressing the gathering, he was among a small group of delegates granted a private audience with Pope Francis. In a striking gesture, the Pope asked Zikode to pray for him. The encounter was deeply symbolic: a recognition of the dignity and centrality of popular movements in the struggle for justice, and an affirmation that their voices carried global moral authority.

As the movement's global links continued to grow, its leaders affirmed their commitment to participate in the construction of a global left on the basis of equality, and not merely to receive solidarity from the North. Speaking in Oslo on 24 November 2016, Thapelo Mohapi said: "We are committed to a society and a world in which land, wealth and power are shared on an equal basis." His intervention affirmed that grassroots movements in the Global South are not only sites of resistance, but also, at their best, sites of democratic imagination and global solidarity.

Repression escalates and Zikode goes underground

The year 2017 got off to a promising start as the movement launched its first village structure, in KwaMzize in Bizana, in the Eastern Cape. However, repression escalated, and four lives were lost during the year.

On 29 May residents of Foreman Road organised road blockades. After attacking the blockades the police attacked the settlement with batons, rubber bullets and teargas. Homes filled with smoke, children were left choking and vomiting, and two-week-old Jayden Khoza died after inhaling the gas. His parents carried his body to the Sydenham police station in protest.

On 13 June Samuel Hloele, aged 29, was shot dead by the Municipal Anti-Land Invasion Unit during evictions in eMasenseni, now called eKukhanyeni, near Marianhill.

On 19 November Sibonelo Patrick Mpeku, chairperson of the Sisonke Village branch in Lamontville, was kidnapped from his home and murdered. He was 32 years old and had long faced threats as a result of his defence of community land rights.

On 17 December Soyiso Nkqayini, Youth League organiser at the eNkanini occupation in Cato Manor, was shot dead inside the settlement. His comrade Smanga Mkhize was seriously injured in the same attack.

On 22 May S'fiso Ngcobo, chairperson of the eKukhanyeni branch in Marianhill, was shot dead in his home after repeated threats. He was killed just days after leading a branch meeting. His assassination followed a now-familiar pattern in which local leaders who resisted party control or opposed corruption were threatened and then murdered.

In the immediate aftermath of the assassination, threats

against the leadership escalated sharply. There were public threats and high-level, detailed warnings of an imminent assassination attempt on S'bu Zikode. He went completely underground, cutting all cell phone contact and even severing communication with his family, relying on a very small circle of comrades for safety. He moved from one safe house to another, living in secrecy, with the knowledge that armed men were actively looking for him. The strategy was not just to take his life but also to break his connection with the movement: the aim was to eliminate his influence by making him invisible. Intelligence officials approached him through intermediaries, offering protection on condition that he cooperate, testify against the ANC's mayor, and go into witness protection in Cape Town. S'bu refused, judging this to be a strategy of political neutralisation. For months he lived in isolation, completely underground, unable to appear in public, carrying the burden of personal danger and isolation along with enforced separation from the movement.

On 26 August 2018, Inkosi Thulani Mjanyelwa was murdered outside his home in Dindini Village, Mbizana by a mob. A respected leader in Mpondoland, he had stood firmly against the sale of land in the interests of an alliance between mining companies and political elites. On 4 August, he had joined other traditional leaders in publicly welcoming Abahlali's presence in emaMpondweni and affirming that the land must remain with the people.

A compromised leadership is recalled

While Zikode was in hiding, an internal crisis came to a head. A group of three leaders, all of them former members of the Kennedy Road Development Committee (KRDC), had aligned themselves with the ANC in Durban, with Nafupa-SA, the undertakers' association close to Jacob Zuma, and with the Zuma aligned and rampantly corrupt VBS Mutual Bank. VBS presented its "loans" as business opportunities, but in reality these were bribes for political support.

Together with Nafupa-SA, the plan was to turn Abahlali's mass membership into a base for a funeral business backed by VBS, binding the movement into ANC patronage networks. This was a direct attempt to capture the movement, to subordinate it to party politics, and to convert it into a source of personal wealth for a few individuals. These men had used their positions to protect the ANC, to silence criticism of the party at public events, to frustrate growth in Gauteng and the Eastern Cape, to order the Abahlali choir to sing at an ANC function, and to centralise decisions in the office rather than in open assemblies.

On 16 September 2018 a Special General Assembly was convened in Durban to confront the crisis. Hundreds of members attended, and for the first time since going underground Zikode appeared in public, welcomed with deep emotion. Thapelo Mohapi, the General Secretary, opened with Amílcar Cabral's famous words: "Hide nothing from the masses of our people. Tell no lies. Expose lies whenever they are told. Mask no difficulties, mistakes, failures." The Assembly concluded that the actions of the three men were a serious threat to democracy in the movement, and to its principles and autonomy. After full debate, it was resolved to dissolve both the KwaZulu-Natal Provincial Council and the National Council, and to elect a new leadership within 30 days. An Interim Committee of five – S'bu Zikode, Mqapheli Bonono, Thapelo Mohapi, Zanele Mtshali and Nomnikelo Sigenu – was chosen to oversee the process.

This was deemed the most democratic way forward: all leaders, whether implicated or not, would have to return to the members and seek a fresh mandate. The Assembly made its resolutions public. In this way, nothing was hidden and the right to recall was exercised in its most serious form since the founding of the movement. The attempt at capture was defeated transparently and democratically. The right to recall leaders via open assembly had saved the movement

S'bu Zikode is carried back into public life

In the weeks that followed, mobilisation grew toward a mass protest on 8 October. Led by Mqapheli Bonono, some five thousand members – joined by organised migrants, street traders and trade unions – marched from Curries Fountain to the Durban City Hall under a heavy police presence. There was international solidarity too, with parallel actions in Cape Town, Johannesburg and New York. Mid-march Mqapheli Bonono warned, "If the City continues not to take us seriously, we will no longer have a legal march... we will do more." At the City Hall, S'bu Zikode, appearing in public for the first time in months, asked, "Why are we being killed by our own for wanting land and development?" It was an extraordinary moment in which the movement demonstrated its resilience and power in a way that reopened public space for its leadership. After the march S'bu Zikode was able to return to public life.

During the course of 2018 the movement had been saddened by Mnikelo Ndabankulu's turn to xenophobic politics. He had left the movement in 2017, after coming under severe pressure from his family. After some time out of the movement he began to regularly make distressing and alarming xenophobic statements on social media and began to publicly attack the movement. On 18 October 2018, he was invited by Niren Tolsi to speak at the Ruth First Lecture – a lecture named in honour of a communist martyr – at the University of the Witwatersrand despite his regular and public xenophobic statements. He is currently a leader in an ANC branch.

On 7 December, Abahlali announced that the Interim Committee that had been appointed after the recall of the leadership would hand over responsibility for elections to an independent body. A special congress was held and a new leadership elected with independent oversight.

eKhenana

The eKhenana occupation in Cato Crest was first established in August 2018, when people who had been made homeless by a corrupt housing project, together with backyard dwellers and young people needing homes of their own, moved onto a piece of unused municipal land. From the outset there was serious tension in the new occupation: some sought to buy, sell and rent land and shacks for profit, while others insisted that land should not be commodified but held in common. There was no formal organisation, no agreed system of self-management, and no clear set of political principles to govern life in the settlement.

The occupation came under immediate and repeated attack from the eThekwini Municipality's Land Invasion Unit, often accompanied by private security, police, and the local ANC councillor Mzi Ngiba. Demolitions were frequent and violent, accompanied by teargas, beatings and even live ammunition. Residents were regularly injured, but rebuilt each time after their homes were destroyed.

In early 2019, the occupiers turned to Abahlali baseMjondolo for support. With the help of SERI, they secured an interdict from the Durban High Court on 13 February 2019 preventing further demolitions. Although the municipality often ignored court orders, the judgment gave residents a foothold from which to continue to build the occupation. On 27 December 2019, a further urgent interdict was granted, again restraining the municipality and its Land Invasion Unit from carrying out evictions or demolitions at eKhenana.

On 14 April 2019, the eKhenana branch of Abahlali base-Mjondolo was formally launched, marked by the slaughter of a cow in celebration. But the underlying tensions soon sharpened. A small group continued to pursue the commodification of land and resisted consensus-based decision-making, while others sought to establish a democratic, collective way of life. There were also serious allegations of abuse, including against women. In September 2019, Abahlali suspended the branch, terminating its membership and advising that residents resolve the issues openly in the community before reapplying for affiliation.

Despite these difficulties, 2019 was decisive: eKhenana survived waves of violent repression, secured its first legal protections, and began the process of transforming itself from a fragile and divided occupation into what would later become a commune organised around collective production and political education.

In 2020 eKhenana was subjected to repeated violent evictions by the eThekwini Municipality's Anti-Land Invasion Unit. On 24 April the Durban High Court granted an interdict prohibiting further demolitions, but the municipality continued to act in contempt of court. Shortly afterwards, during another attempt to carry out an eviction, an Anti-Land Invasion Unit officer named Mkhize opened fire with live ammunition on residents. One person, Yamkela Vezi, was seriously injured. These attacks followed on from the previous year's attempts to destroy the occupation, and made clear the determination of both the City and the local ANC to prevent eKhenana from taking root.

March for the Decommodification of Land

On 24 February 2019 thousands of Abahlali members, together with street traders, hostel dwellers and workers, gathered outside the Durban City Hall to march for the total decommodification of land. The movement came to the march with more than seventy ongoing occupations and a membership approaching 80,000.

The call for total decommodification was the outcome of months of debate across the branches and occupations, as people reflected on their daily experience of dispossession and violent eviction, and on the limits of state-led reform. These discussions crystallised around the demand that land be recognised not as a commodity, but as a public good to be allocated on the basis of human need and managed collectively from below. The principle of umhlaba noma ukufa – land or death – had regularly arisen in branch discussions for years.

The march was timed to coincide with the final days for submissions to Parliament on the proposed legislation to enable expropriation without compensation. Abahlali rejected the elite consensus that such a process should simply transfer land from white elites to black elites, insisting instead that land must be taken out of the market entirely, constitutionalised as a right, and governed through democratic structures rooted in communities. The memorandum stressed that the state could not be trusted to administer land fairly, given its record of corruption, authoritarianism and violence, and that only popular democratic power could make such a right meaningful.

The content of the demands was sweeping. Abahlali called for all evictions to be made illegal, for the state to respond to land occupations with support, including the provision of infrastructure, rather than armed repression, for women to have full and equal access to land, and for both urban and rural land – residential, agricultural, and commercial – to be brought under collective, democratic control.

It stood as the most comprehensive articulation of Abahlali's land politics since its founding, less a protest statement than a manifesto distilled from 15 years of struggle in occupations, the streets, political education workshops and courts. The march marked a high point in Abahlali's ability to take grassroots analysis, forged through years of direct confrontation with the state, into the national debate on land reform. It made clear that for the movement, decommodification was not an abstract demand but a lived principle, already practised in occupations, and advanced at real risk of eviction, assault, imprisonment, and assassination.

In November Melita Ngcobo, a powerful leader in Gauteng, was arrested in Vusimuzi, Thembisa, during a struggle against evictions. The community had already secured a High Court interdict protecting them from evictions, but municipal officials and police returned to the settlement and continued to destroy people's homes. Melita confronted them directly, demanding that they obey the court order and stop the demolitions. In response, she was insulted, assaulted and arrested. She later successfully sued the police for damages.

By 2021 eKhenana was functioning as a working commune. A number of projects had been built: a communal kitchen and tuck-shop, a poultry project, and a vegetable garden, along with a community hall and the Frantz Fanon Political School. These projects were named in honour of assassinated comrades – the garden for Nkululeko Gwala, the poultry project for S'fiso Ngcobo, the hall for Thuli Ndlovu – so that the commune combined collective life with living memory. The commune was a practical response to everyday needs, and at the same time a deliberate experiment in decommodified, socialist forms of life – an experiment that would later be replicated in other occupations.

The Per Anger Prize & more repression

On 25 March 2021 it was announced that S'bu Zikode would receive the Per Anger Prize, the Swedish Government's official award for human rights and democracy, in recognition of his leadership of Abahlali baseMjondolo and the struggle for land, housing and dignity in shack settlements. In his acceptance speech on 21 April, he declared that "the price for land and dignity has been paid in blood," insisting that shack dwellers "are not criminals, we are not less than human," and that the struggle was not against people but "against an unjust system." He dedicated the award to comrades assassinated in the struggle, including Thuli Ndlovu and Nkululeko Gwala, saying it belonged to all who had fallen. He added that while he continued to live "in the shadow of death," the award gave some protection because "the world is watching."

On 6 May 2021 Abahlali's deputy president, Mqapheli Bonono, was arrested on false charges at the movement's offices in Durban. He was charged with conspiracy to murder after chairing a community meeting to establish the facts around a murder and the arrests that had followed. He was detained at the Durban Central Police Station before being transferred to Westville Prison. Bail was denied twice and he faced threats of violence inside prison. At the time of his arrest, other leaders from eKhenana – Lindokuhle Mnguni, Ayanda Ngila, Landu Shazi and Maphiwe Gasela – were already in Westville Prison, having been held there for months after being denied bail. The men organised a reading group studying Fanon and other texts line by line, in the manner that Mqapehli Bonono had learnt from the MST, turning the prison into a site of collective learning and political formation.

In July 2021, KwaZulu-Natal and Gauteng erupted into riots that left hundreds dead and caused enormous destruction. While many commentators framed the unrest as a political intervention in support of Jacob Zuma, Abahlali insisted that it was, at its core, a rebellion driven by hunger and desperation. In a statement issued on 13 July, the movement argued that "poverty and hunger were a bomb and the breakdown in order caused by Zuma's people lit the fuse." Abahlali noted that for a few days the unrest took the form of a mass food riot by the poor, and while many took food, they did not burn or destroy and that the large-scale destruction that came later was driven by other forces with political agendas. The movement insisting that the underlying crisis of mass poverty had to be addressed if South Africa was to avoid further chaos.

The repression concentrated on eKhenana reached a terrible intensity in 2022, with the systematic assassination of its elected leadership.

On 8 March 2022, Ayanda Ngila, the deputy chairperson of the commune, was shot dead in broad daylight while repairing a water pipe in the food gardens. His killing followed years of arrests on fabricated charges and a long campaign of intimidation directed at the Commune.

On 5 May, just two months later, Nokuthula Mabaso, a leading woman in eKhenana and head of the Women's League, was assassinated outside her home in front of her children. She had played a central role in defending the Commune and was also a key state witness in Ngila's case. In the days before her assassination she had identified suspects and made an affidavit against Khaya Ngubane, a local ANC Youth League member.

Samson Ngubane, Khaya's father, and Mhlanganyelwa Ngubane, his uncle – both also linked to the local ANC – were arrested. The movement was explicit that it "condemned the killing of any person by any person" and emphasised the need for a full legal process in which justice had to be pursued carefully and transparently, with all facts brought to light in court.

On 20 August, Lindokuhle Mnguni, chairperson of eKhenana and national chairperson of Abahlali, was murdered in his home. He had already endured repeated arrests, months in prison, and numerous threats. Mnguni was widely recognised as a central thinker in the movement. He was deeply involved in the socialist experiment at eKhenana and had introduced the slogan Socialism or Death, insisting that socialism had to be lived in the present, not deferred to a distant future. He also composed the song Sizozabalaza ("We will struggle"), which became popular across the movement as a whole. Both the slogan and the song captured the best of the spirit of the commune and carried intense emotional resonance after his death.

The three assassinations in less than six months were a coordinated attempt to destroy the commune's leadership as the local ANC, the municipality, and local business interests worked together to crush autonomous forms of life outside commodification.

On 15 March 2023, Khaya Ngubane was convicted in the Durban High Court for the assassination of Ayanda Ngila, who had been murdered at eKhenana on 8 March 2022. He was sentenced on 17 March 2023 to fifteen years' imprisonment.

By this time new Communes were being built in Gauteng and KwaZulu-Natal.

The People's Minimum Demands

On 26 April 2023, more than 10,000 people marched from Curries Fountain to Durban City Hall to mark UnFreedom Day. For the first time, the day was observed in three provinces: KwaZulu-Natal (Durban, 26 April), Mpumalanga (Volksrust, 28 April), and Gauteng (Germiston, 29 April). The Durban march culminated in the delivery of a memorandum of 16 demands to the Presidency. These included an end to assassinations, evictions, transit camps, and loadshedding; the creation of jobs; and support for street traders and taxi workers. The memorandum also expressed clear and principled opposition to xenophobia, sexism, and homophobia.

In its statement, Abahlali stressed that poor people remained unfree because they continued to face assassination, police violence, the destruction of their homes, the denial of urban land, and forced relocation to transit camps. It noted that democracy had been won by the struggles of ordinary people and is defended today by those same struggles, not by politicians. The speeches on the steps of City Hall emphasised the building of communes, the decommodification of land and housing, and the defence of dignity and humanity against "fake freedom." While the march centred on land, housing, and dignity, S'bu Zikode's closing speech placed particular emphasis on solidarity with Palestine.

In advance of the 29 May 2024 general election, Abahlali initiated a movement-wide process on 3 February 2024 to develop a set of People's Minimum Demands. Over the following weeks, thousands of members participated in hundreds of meetings across all structures, including the Women's League and Youth League, as well as open General Assemblies. Three principles guided the discussions: that the ANC's repression and assassinations had to be confronted at the ballot; that there was no left party on the ballot; and that abstention was not viable, requiring a purely tactical vote against the ANC and MK, with no possibility of voting for the DA. A voter-registration drive was also undertaken to ensure members were prepared to act collectively.

From 22 to 24 March, a national leadership camp held in the Valley of a Thousand Hills finalised the People's Minimum Demands and resolved to invite parties – excluding the ANC, MK, and DA – to a General Assembly on 7 April to respond. At that Assembly, several parties engaged with the demands, and by the close of the process one party agreed to commit clearly on key issues including land, education, and Palestine.

On 21 April, at a huge UnFreedom Day rally at the eNkanini Sports Ground in Durban attended by around 20,000 people, the movement announced that it would cast a tactical vote for the Economic Freedom Fighters, conditional on their commitment to the People's Minimum Demands. The announcement emphasised that this was a tactical decision taken in the context of an election, that Abahlali remained independent and autonomous, and concluded: "On 29 May we will vote. On 30 May we will continue the struggle."

By the end of the year the movement's membership had grown to more than 150,000 across 93 branches in four provinces. Branches membership has to be renewed through elections and on 1 January 2024, the membership of the eKhenana branch formally lapsed after failing to hold elections. Repression always results in trauma and anxiety and can sometimes result in paranoia and serious divisions in movements. People who have suffered serious repression can come to feel that they should have a special standing in a movement, a standing above democratic processes. In this context, two factions emerged within the community, democratic practices broke down, and elections were not held when due. Serious complaints were made about a small group of residents. Under these conditions the branch could no longer sustain the collective democratic practices required for renewal.

In September and October, a series of assemblies were held to begin the work of rebuilding unity in eKhenana. On 10 November, an open assembly attended by 54 residents was opened by S'bu Zikode with the words: "We are here to bring peace, unity and stability." A large majority signed a declaration committing to peace, while a small faction held out. The meeting marked a first step in a longer process of healing after years in which the community had faced both severe repression and internal strain.

On 25 April, more than 10,000 people marched from Curries Fountain to the Durban City Hall to mark UnFreedom Day, where the movement reaffirmed its core demand that land, wealth, and power must be fairly shared, and that democracy must mean the day-to-day power of the people. Solidarity was expressed for struggles in Palestine, the Congo, Swaziland, and elsewhere. At the same time, rallies were also held in Gauteng and Mpumalanga on 27 April, despite police attempts to ban the Mpumalanga rally on the spurious grounds that President Cyril Ramaphosa was speaking nearby. The movement defied the ban.

On 19 July the eKhenana branch was relaunched after a successful reconstitution of democratic practices.

Confronting Fascism

Later in the year, the movement was compelled to directly confront Operation Dudula, a fascist formation built on anti-migrant hatred and scapegoating. Dudula had mounted aggressive campaigns at hospitals, blocking migrants from accessing healthcare, and sought to extend its attacks by threatening organisations that defended migrants, including SERI.

The issue was discussed at the General Assembly in Durban and in all the Johannesburg branches. When Operation Dudula marched on the offices of SERI on 17 July they arrived to find that they were vastly outnumbered by comrades from the movement. They were humiliated by the dignified, determined presence of the movement and had to leave in disgrace. The mobilisation outside SERI reaffirmed Abahlali's long-standing principle that a person is a person wherever they may find themselves, and that the struggles of the poor must never be turned against each other but against the real systems of exploitation and repression.

It was very sad that in the same week that the movement had confronted Operation Dudula in Johannesburg Mnikelo Ndabankulu, the former leader who had left the movement in 2017, was working with March and March – another xenophobic organisation – to block people from accessing a public hospital in Durban.

Challenges, Victories and Lessons

Over the past twenty years Abahlali baseMjondolo has had to confront serious challenges including regular violence. The movement emerged from undignified, dangerous and often life-threatening conditions in shack settlements, from social abandonment and political domination. People were living with regular shack fires, floods, disease along with police harassment and a national liberation movement that was now, in the words of Frantz Fanon, trying to 'hold the people down'. The movement emerged from the failure of the ANC to reallocate urban land on the basis of social need rather than private profit. It emerged in opposition to the ANC's project of destroying shack settlements and either leaving people homeless or forcing them, often at gunpoint, to desolate human dumping grounds far from the cities.

The movement had to fight and fight hard to democratise shack settlements that had been run by unelected committees, party appointed leaders or izinduna. It had to fight for the right to organise outside of the ANC, to be able to speak freely to the media, to use the courts and to organise protests. At the same time it had to struggle to assert its autonomy from NGOs and factions of the donor supported middle class left that assumed a right to rule the struggles of the poor.

The ANC, the state and some liberal and left NGOs all saw the emergence of an autonomous movement of the poor as a threat to their power. Actors in all of these forces sought to buy influence over the movement and to criminalise it – to rule it or ruin it. Today the movement regularly and freely organises large marches and rallies of thousands of people and it is a constant presence in the media.

The movement is also able to directly resist eviction, organise road blockades and marches, and make regular tactical use of the courts. We have won numerous victories in the courts, including many interdicts, and a landmark case in the Constitutional Court.

A high price was paid for these political victories, including slander, job losses, the destruction of people's homes, arrests, assaults, torture and murder. There was a widespread inability to understand that poor black people can think and speak for ourselves and the movement was repeatedly slandered as 'orchestrated' by a white man and as a plot by foreign governments. When state repression failed to break the movement ethnic and xenophobic violence were deployed against it, along with ongoing attempts at capture and co-option.

The movement has also won many material victories and made many social advances. It has successfully defended many thousands of people against evictions, and won large amounts of new land. It has provided self-organised access to services to occupations, such as water and electricity. It has developed new forms of democratic self-governance in communes and assemblies.

The movement defeated the attempt to 'eradicate' shacks and won a turn towards upgrading shack settlements. Government provided services such as water, electricity and sanitation have been won. Abahlali has compelled the eThekwini Municipality to build houses in Kennedy Road, Parkgate, Cornubia, Salt Rock, and other settlements.

It has not only survived oppression through the police and other armed forces contracted by the state as well as the repression by local councillors, ward committees, party structures and the izinkabi. It has also held the forces of repression to account by mobilising international solidarity and winning damages against the police and convictions for murder, including against a police officer, local party thugs, a hired assassin and two ANC councillors.

The movement always insisted that every branch must be run democratically in order to sustain its membership. In recent years it has gone beyond this initial requirement and also worked to turn occupations into productive communes with political schools, community halls and other social infrastructure, as well the production of healthy food.

We have built strong relations with comrades and movements across the world and are working to build a movement of communes and a global movement of movements. We have taken a leading role in opposing ethnic and xenophobic politics, in working to build unity between the poor and the working class and supporting migrants, hostel dwellers, street traders and others to organise themselves and build their own organisations. We have also collaborated with many progressive organisations, groups representing sex workers, taking up environmental issues, and many more.

We have also trained many people in computer and media skills, supported many young people to obtain drivers' licences and undertaken various kinds of training and support through the Youth and Women's Leagues.

From a movement that began with a meeting of 32 people in Durban on 4 October 2005 with we now have more than 180,000 members in more than 100 branches in four provinces.

Through all of this, Abahlali has remained a people's movement, a space of dignity and a source of pride and hope. The movement has drawn important lessons from twenty years of struggle. Building solidarity between and within struggling communities is essential, as is the affirmation of the dignity of all people. Leadership must be carried out with humility and respect for the intelligence of every member. Collectivism must be given priority over individualism. The principles of ubuhlali and ubuntu remain foundational to our struggle. Learning from one another's experiences has been a constant source of strength, and political education has played a central role. Strategic alliances and collaborations have been identified and cultivated, and international solidarity built. Abahlali has always defended its autonomy against capture or distortion by external forces, and has refused to be captured by NGOs or political parties.

Democratic and courageous leadership has been affirmed as vital. Above all, the movement has learnt the importance of consolidating the broader unity of the poor and the working class through principled struggle and the building of life-affirming institutions from below.

Forward to the next twenty years of building the democratic power of the oppressed from below!

Movement Documents for Further Reading

We are the Third Force

First published in the Daily News *in November 2005, this article by S'bu Zikode – the first to be published by a member of the movement – caused a national sensation. It confronted the claim, widespread at the time across the elites in the state, the ANC, the media, NGOs and the universities that the movement must really be 'orchestrated' by a white man – a very old racist idea about black movements for freedom.*

1. We are the Third Force
S'bu Zikode

The shack dwellers' movement that has given hope to thousands of people in Durban is always being accused of being part of the Third Force. In newspapers and in all kinds of meetings this is said over and over again. They even waste money investigating the Third Force. We need to address this question of the Third Force so that people don't become confused.

I must warn those comrades, government officials, politicians and intellectuals who speak about the Third Force that they have no idea what they are talking about. They are too high to really feel what we feel. They always want to talk for us and about us, but they must allow us to talk about our lives and our struggles.

We need to get things clear. There definitely is a Third Force. The question is what is it and who is part of the Third Force? Well, I am Third Force myself. The Third Force is all the pain and the suffering that the poor are subjected to every second in our lives. The shack dwellers have many things to say about the Third Force. It is time for us to speak out and to say this is who we are, this is where we are and this how we live. The life that we are living makes our communities the Third Force. Most of us are not working and have to spend all day struggling for small money. AIDS is worse in the shack settlements than anywhere else. Without proper houses, water, electricity, refuse removal and toilets all kinds of diseases breed. The causes are clearly visible and every Dick, Tom and Harry can understand. Our bodies itch every day because of the insects. If it is raining everything is wet – blankets and floors. If it is hot the mosquitoes and flies are always there. There is no holiday in the shacks. When the evening comes – it is always a challenge. The night is supposed to be for relaxing and getting rest. But it doesn't happen like that in the jondolos. People stay awake worrying about their lives. You must see how big the rats are that will run across the small babies in the night. You must see how people have to sleep under the bridges when it rains because their floors are so wet. The rain comes right inside people's houses. Some people just stand up all night.

But poverty is not just suffering. It threatens us with death every day. We have seen how dangerous being poor is. In the Kennedy Road settlement, we have seen how Mhlengi Khumalo, a one-year-old child, died in a shack fire last month. Seven others have died in fires since the eThekwini Metro decided to stop providing electricity to informal settlements. There are many Mhlengis all over our country. Poverty even threatens people in flats. In Bayview, in Chatsworth, a woman died of hunger earlier this year – she was fearing to tell the neighbours that she had no food. She died alone.

Those in power are blind to our suffering. This is because they have not seen what we see, they have not felt what we are feeling every second, every day. My appeal is that leaders who are concerned about peoples' lives must come and stay at least one week in the jondolos. They must feel the mud. They must share 6 toilets with 6,000 people. They must dispose of their own refuse while living next to the dump. They must come with us while we look for work. They must chase away the rats and keep the children from knocking the candles. They must care for the sick when there are long queues for the tap. They must have a turn to explain to the children why they can't attend the Technical College down the hill. They must be there when we bury our children who have passed on in the fires, from diarrhoea or AIDS.

For us the most important struggle is to be recognised as human beings. During the struggle prior to 1994 there were only two levels, two classes – the rich and the poor. Now after the election there are three classes – the poor, the middle class and the rich. The poor have been isolated from the middle class. We are becoming more poor and the rest are becoming more rich. We are on our own. We are completely on our own.

Our President Mbeki speaks politics – our Premier Ndebele, and Shilowa in Gauteng and Rasool in the Western Cape, our Mayor Mlaba and mayors all over the country speak politics. But who will speak about the genuine issues that affect the people every day – water, electricity, education, land, housing? We thought local government would minimise politics and focus on what people need but it all becomes politics.

We discovered that our municipality does not listen to us when we speak to them in Zulu. We tried English. Now we realise that they won't understood Xhosa or Sotho either. The only language that they understand is when we put thousands of people on the street. We have seen the results of this, and we have been encouraged. It works very well. It is the only tool that we have to emancipate our people. Why should we stop it?

We have matured in our suffering. We had a programme to find a way forward. Our programme was to continue with the peaceful negotiations with the authorities that first started ten years ago. But our first plan was undermined. We were lied to. We had to come up with an alternative plan.

16 February 2005 was the dawn of our struggle. On that day the Kennedy Road committee had a very successful meeting with the chair of the housing portfolio of the executive committee of the municipality, the director of housing and the ward councillor. They all promised us the vacant land on the Clare Estate for housing. The land on Elf Road was one of the identified areas. But then we were betrayed by the most trusted people in our city. Just one month later, without any warning or explanation, bulldozers began digging the land. People were excited. They went to see what was happening and were shocked to be told that a brick factory was

being built there. Later, when we blocked the road, our local councillor, a man put into power by our votes and holding our trust and hopes, told the police "Arrest these people – they are criminals." The police beat us, their dogs bit us and they arrested 14 of us. We asked what happened to the promised land. We were told "Who the hell are you people to demand this land?" This betrayal mobilised the people. The people who betrayed us are responsible for this movement. Those people are the second force.

Our movement started with 14 arrests – we called them the 14 heroes. Now we have 14 settlements united together as Abahlali baseMjondolo [shack dwellers]. Each settlement meets once a week, and the leaders of all the settlements meet once a week. We are prepared to talk but if that doesn't work we are prepared to use our strength. We will do whatever it costs us to get what we need to live safely.

We have learnt from our experience that when you want to achieve what you want, when you want to achieve what is legitimate by peaceful negotiations, by humbleness, by respecting those in authority your plea becomes criminal. You will be deceived for more than ten years, you will be fooled and undermined. This is why we have resorted to the streets. When we stand there in our thousands we are taken seriously.

The struggle that started in Kennedy Road was the beginning of a new era. We are aware of the strategies that the police are coming with to demoralise and threaten the poor. We don't mind them building the jails for us and hiring more security if they are not prepared to listen to what we are saying. It is important for every shack dwellers to know that we are aware of what is happening in Alexander in Johannesburg, in P.E., in Cape Town. We know that our struggle is not by itself. We have sent our solidarity. We will not rest in peace until there is justice for the poor – not only in Kennedy Road there are many Kennedy Roads, many Mhlengis, many poor voices that are not heard and not understood. But we have discovered the language that works. We will stick with it. The victims have spoken. We have said enough is enough.

It must be clear that this is not a political game. This movement is a kind of social tool by which the community hopes to get quicker results. This has nothing to do with politics or parties. Our members are part of every political organisation that you may think of. This is a non-political movement. It will finish its job when land and housing, electricity and basic services have been won and poverty eliminated. It is enough for us to be united until our people have achieved what is wanted – which is basic. But until that is materialised we will never stop.

The community has realised that voting for parties has not brought any change to us – especially at the level of local government elections. We can see some important changes at national level but at local level whoever wins the elections will be challenged by us. We have been betrayed by our own elected councillor. We have decided not to vote. The campaign that has begun – 'No Land, No House, No Vote', is a campaign that has been agreed upon in all 14 settlements.

We are driven by the Third Force, the suffering of the poor. Our betrayers are the Second Force. The First Force was our struggle against apartheid. The Third Force will stop when the Fourth Force comes. The Fourth Force is land, housing, water, electricity, health care, education and work. We are only asking what is basic – not what is luxurious. This is the struggle of the poor. The time has come for the poor to show themselves that we can be poor in life but not in mind.

For us time has been a very good teacher. People have realised so many things. We have learnt from the past – we have suffered alone. That pain and suffering has taught us a lot. We have begun to realise that we are not supposed to be living under these conditions. There has been a dawn of democracy for the poor. No one else would have told us – neither our elected leaders nor any officials would have told us what we are entitled to. Even the Freedom Charter is only good in theory. It has nothing to do with the ordinary lives of poor. It doesn't help us. It is the thinking of the masses of the people that matters. We have noted that our country is rich. More airports are being built, there are more developments at the Point water front, more stadiums are being renovated, more money is floating around, even being lent to Mugabe. But when you ask for what is basic you are told that there is no money. It is clear that there is no money for the poor. The money is for the rich. We have come to the decision of saying 'enough is enough.' We all agree that something must be done.

2. Eliminate the Slums Act

21 June 2007

Abahlali baseMjondolo Press Statement

Operation Murambatsvina comes to KZN:
The Notorious Elimination & Prevention of
Re-emergence of Slums Bill

Today the KwaZulu-Natal Elimination & Prevention of Re-emergence of Slums Bill will be tabled in the provincial parliament. Abahlali baseMjondolo have discussed this Bill very carefully in many meetings. We have heard Housing MEC Mike Mabuyakulu say that we must not worry because it is aimed at slumlords and shack farming. We have heard Ranjith Purshotum from the Legal Resources Centre say that "Instead of saying that people will be evicted from slums after permanent accommodation is secured, we have a situation where people are being removed from a slum, and sent to another slum. Only this time it is a government-approved slum and is called a transit area. This is the twisted logic of the drafters of the legislation". We have heard Marie Huchzermeyer from Wits University say that this Bill uses the language of apartheid, is anti-poor and is in direct contradiction with the national housing policy Breaking New Ground. Lawyers have told us that this Bill is unconstitutional.

It is very clear to us that this Bill is an attempt to mount a legal attack on the poor. Already the poor, shack dwellers and street traders, are under illegal and violent attack by municipalities. This Bill is an attempt to legalize the attacks on the poor. We know about Operation Murambatsvina. Last year one of our members visited Harare and last week we hosted two people from Harare. This Bill is an attempt to legalize a KZN Operation Murambatsvina before the World Cup in 2010. We will fight it all the way.

1. Aim of the Bill

The Bill says that its main aims are to:

- Eliminate 'slums' in KwaZulu-Natal
- Prevent new 'slums' from developing
- Upgrade and control existing 'slums'
- Monitor the performance of departments and municipalities in the elimination of 'slums' and the prevention of new 'slums' from developing.

It has detailed plans to make sure that all of this really happens. The Bill also says that it aims to 'improve the living conditions of communities' but it has no detailed plans to make sure that this really happens. It is therefore clear that its real purpose is to get rid of 'slums' rather than to improve the conditions in which people live. Mabuyakulu says that we shouldn't worry because the real targets are slum lords and shack farming but this is not what the Bill says and, anyway, there are no slum lords in Abahlali settlements. Abahlali members have been to Nairobi. We have seen how the slum lords rule the Nairobi settlements and we are strongly against slum lordism. But we do not live in Nairobi. All Abahlali settlements are democratic communities and many other settlements in KZN are also not run by slum lords.

The Bill does not aim to:

- Force local and provincial government to deal with the conditions that force people to leave their homes and move to shack settlements

- Force local and provincial government to immediately provide basic services to shack settlements like toilets, electricity, water, drainage, paths and speed bumps while they wait for upgrades or relocations

- Force local and provincial government to follow the laws that prevent evictions without a court order, the laws that prevent people from being made homeless in an eviction or to follow the Breaking New Ground Policy that aims to upgrade settlements in situ (where people are already living) instead of relocating people so far from work and schools that they have to leave their low cost houses and come straight back to shacks.

- Force local and provincial government to make their plans for shack dwellers with shack dwellers to avoid the bad planning that undermines development (such as relocating people so far away from work that they have to move back to shacks)

We do not need this Bill. The first thing that we need is for government (local, provincial and national) to begin to follow the existing laws and polices that protect against evictions, forced relocations and which recommend in situ upgrades instead of relocations. After that we need laws that break the power that the very rich have over land in the cities and we need laws to compel municipalities to provide services to shack settlements while people wait for houses to be built.

This Bill is not for shack dwellers. It is to protect the rich, by protecting their property prices.

2. Definition of imijondolo

In the Bill the word 'slum' is defined as an overcrowded piece of land or building where poor people live and where there is poor or no infrastructure or toilets.

The Bill uses the word 'slum' in a way that makes it sound like the places where poor people live are a problem that must be cleared away because there is something wrong with poor people. But it does not admit that the poor have been made poor but the same history of theft and exploitation that made the rich to be rich and it does not admit that places where poor people live often lack infrastructure and toilets because of the failure of landlords or the government to provide these things. The solution to the fact that we often don't have toilets in our communities is to provide toilets where we live and not to destroy our communities and move us out of the city. In this Bill the word 'slum' is used to make it sound like the poor and the places where they live are the problem rather than the rich and the way in which they have made the poor to be poor and to be kept poor by a lack of development.

In America black community organizations have opposed the use of the word 'slum' to describe their communities because they say it makes it sound like there is something wrong with them and their places rather than the system that makes them poor and fails to develop their places. They also say that once a place is called a 'slum' it is easy to for the rich and governments to say that it must be 'cleared' or 'eliminated' but if a place is called a community then it is easier to say that it must be supported and developed.

There is also a problem with calling imijondolo 'informal settlements' because once a place is called 'informal' it is easy for people to say that it shouldn't get any of the 'formal' services that people need for a proper life like electricity, toilets, refuse collection and so on. But many of us have lived our whole lives in 'informal settlements'. We can't wait until we live in 'formal' houses to get electricity to stop the fires, water, toilets, drainage, refuse collection and so on. We are living our lives now. We can't wait to start living only when and if the government puts us in a 'formal' one roomed 'house' far out of town.

And we don't like the word 'eliminate'. This is a word that is violent and threatening, not respectful and caring. Our communities should be nurtured, not eliminated.

The people who live in the imijondolo must decide for themselves what they want their communities to be called. We must be allowed to define ourselves and to speak for ourselves.

3. Supporting the Rich Against the Poor

The Bill makes it criminal to occupy a building or land without permission from the owner of the building or the land.

- It forces municipalities to force landowners to evict people on their land (or in their buildings).
- It forces municipalities to seek evictions if landowners fail to do so.
- It forces municipalities to make a plan to eliminate all the 'slums' in its area within six months of this Bill becoming law.
- It forces municipalities to give an annual report on its progress towards eliminating all 'slums'.
- It forces the provincial Department of Housing to closely watch municipalities and to support them to make sure that they evict people from land that they have occupied.
- It forces the Provincial Department of Housing to support 'any project adopted by a municipality' to 'relocate' people from imijondolo.
- It says that Municipalities may evict people when evictions are in the public interest.

- It forces landowners to protect their land against the poor with fences and security guards. Landowners who do not protect their land against the poor will be guilty of a criminal offence.
- It forces landowners to evict people from their land.

This Bill does not provide any protection for people who have been made poor by the same history and economy that made the rich to be rich and who have decided to occupy land or buildings that are owned by the rich but are not being used by them. In many countries the poor have a legal right to use vacant land or buildings that are owned by the rich but are not being used by them. It is like this in Turkey. There is no reason why South Africa can not also give this right to the poor.

The need of the very poor for housing in the cities near work and education should come before the needs of the very rich to have their property prices protected.

4. Transit Areas

The Bill allows Municipalities to buy or take land to accommodate people that have been evicted while they are waiting for new developments. These are called 'transit areas'. The Bill does not give any guaranties as to where these 'transit areas' will be located, what services will be provided there, if communities will be kept together or broken up when people are taken to these places or how long they will have to live in these places.

We know that all through history and in many countries governments have put their political opponents, the very poor, people who were seen as ethnically, cultural and racially different, and people without I.D. books in camps. These camps are always supposed to be temporary – a 'transit' between one place and another. But very often these camps have become places of long and terrible suffering. That is why in the *Mail & Guardian* it was written that this Bill reminds people of Nazi Germany. We know that in India shackdwellers who were taken to transit camps in the 1960s are still there now.

5. Expropriation of Land

The Bill gives Municipalities the right to expropriate land. This means that they have the right to take land from landowners. This could be a very good thing for the poor if land was taken in the cities so that the poor could live safely and legally next to work, schools and clinics. But the Bill says nothing about which land should be taken. It only says that land can be taken to set up a 'transit area' or for people 'removed or evicted from a slum'. Therefore, it seems that the right to expropriate land will most be likely be used to evict the poor from the cities and to dump them in rural areas and not to defend their right to live in the cities against the interests of very rich land speculators and developers. Already shack dwellers are being taken out of Durban and dumped in 'formal' low-cost houses in places like Park Gate. There is no guarantee that this will not continue.

6. Criminalising the Poor

This Bill makes anyone who tries to stop an eviction a criminal who can be fined R20,000 or sent to prison for 5 years. Any normal person would try to stop an eviction. Which mother would stand by while her home and community is destroyed? If this law is passed it will make us all criminals. But this law says nothing about stopping the illegal and unconstitutional evictions that are perpetrated against shackdwellers all the time by the eThekwini Municipality. The Municipality breaks the law every time that it evicts us without a court order and every time it leaves people homeless but Municipal officials are never arrested. If the laws that exist now are not used fairly we have no guarantee that this law will be used fairly.

7. Who Should Plan for the Future of Our Cities?

Durban and Pinetown and Pietermaritzburg and all the cities in this province, this country and in the world were built by the work of the poor. But poor people didn't only build our cities. They have also done a lot of the planning of the development of our cities. It was the poor who decided that black and white and rich and poor shouldn't live separately and who took unused land so that everyone could live together in our cities. Our cities look the way that they do because of both the planning of the rich, the planning of various governments and the planning or ordinary poor people. For example it was Biko Zulu who decided to start a settlement in Jadhu Place near to the schools in Overport and the jobs in Springfield Park and not any government.

A democratic government should allow the poor to continue to be able to participate in planning the future of our cities. Planning should not only be a right for governments and the rich.

On Friday 4 May 2007 the Provincial Legislature came to the Kennedy Road community hall to introduce the "KZN Elimination and Prevention of Re-Emergence of Slums Bill, 2006". The hall was overflowing with people from affiliating settlements of the Abahlali baseMjondolo Movement. We clearly said "No land, No House – No Vote, No Bill!" We clearly told the Provincial Legislature about the illegal demolitions and evictions undertaken by the eThekwini Municipality, the failure to provide basic services to shack dwellers and the brutal criminalization of the politics of the poor by people like Supt. Glen Nayager of the Sydenham Police Station. They said that they do not know about any of this. If they do not know what is happening to shack dwellers in their own province then they must listen to shack dwellers before making laws. Listening and talking must come before deciding.

A World Class city is not a city where the poor are pushed out of the city. A World Class city is a city where the poor are treated with dignity and respect and money is spent on real needs like houses and toilets and clean water and electricity and schools and libraries rather than fancy things for the rich like stadiums and casinos that our cities can just not afford.

We will fight this Bill in the courts. We will fight this Bill in the streets. We will fight this Bill in the way we live our ordinary lives every day. We will not be driven out of our cities as if we were rubbish.

3. A Memorandum of Demands to Mayor Obed Mlaba

The first attempt to march on the mayor in November 2005 was prevented by police violence and arrests. The second, in September 2007, was initially allowed to proceed but then attacked by the police, again resulting in arrests. This memorandum – produced through a careful process of discussion across the movement's branches – conveys the movement's primary concerns in its early years. Because memoranda and press statements were developed collectively and deliberatively, they carried real moral authority. This was central to the movement's capacity to endure and grow through years of sustained police repression.

We the shack dwellers of Durban & Pinetown and our comrades from around the province are democrats and loyal citizens of the Republic of South Africa. We stand here because we are being evicted from our homes and forced off the farms and out of the cities. We stand here because we are dying in shack fires because we do not have electricity. We stand here because we are being raped when we try to find a safe place to go to the toilet in the night. We stand here because we are denied the right to visit the graves of our ancestors. We stand here because in many settlements thousands of people share each tap and toilet. We stand here because children are being forced to stay in their parents' shacks long after they are grown and have their own children. We stand here because we fear that 2010 will be our doom. We stand here because your Municipality breaks the law every time it demolishes our shacks and evicts us without a court order. We stand here because it is clear to us that the rich do not want to give us any space in the cities, in the rural areas or anywhere in the country and that the politicians have decided to be the partners of the rich. We stand here because our councillors do not represent us and so we have to represent ourselves.

The same economy that made the rich to be rich has made the poor to be poor. The wealth in this country was built on the theft of our land and from our work in the farms, mines, factories, kitchens and laundries of the rich. We cannot and will not continue to suffer the way that we do. We cannot and will not allow our voices to be stifled. The time has come for the poor to be heard. The time for politicians to talk for and about the poor while they make deals with the rich is over. The time has come for politicians to talk to the poor and to talk to the poor openly and honestly and respectfully so that we can, together, ensure that there is a place for everyone in this city and in this country.

Mayor Mlaba, today we the shack dwellers of eThekwini make the following demands to you:

- We demand participation in genuinely democratic processes of consultation and citizenship.
- We demand an immediate moratorium on the evictions and demolitions that result in some people being left homeless and others being forcibly removed out of the city.
- We demand adequate land and housing in the city so that we can live in safety, health and dignity.
- We demand an immediate moratorium on the selling of government owned land to private developers

- We demand a commitment to the expropriation of privately owned land for collective, social housing
- We demand an immediate commitment to seriously explore the possibility of upgrading rather than relocating each settlement and to undertake this exploration in partnership with each settlement
- We demand an immediate moratorium on the eviction and harassment of street traders
- We demand that electricity be installed in all shack settlements.
- We demand an adequate supply of well-maintained toilets in all settlements.
- We demand an end to the shortage of taps in our settlements.
- We demand refuse removal in all settlements.
- We demand well-resourced and staffed health facilities and support for our own initiatives to care for people living with HIV/AIDS.
- We demand support for our crèches and an end to the exclusion of our children from schools and universities.
- We are threatened by criminals and we are threatened by police officers who treat us as if we are criminals. We therefore demand policing that respects the poor.
- We demand an immediate recognition that all settlements will experience natural growth, especially as children grow up, and that this requires existing shacks to be expanded and new shacks to be built.
- We demand an immediate explanation as to what happened to the R10 billion Phoenix East housing development that you promised us after we marched on you on 14 November 2005.
- We demand an immediate explanation from you as to what happened to the piece of land adjacent to Loon Road promised to the Foreman Road settlement when you visited the

settlement while campaigning for the 2000 local government elections.

- We demand an immediate explanation from you as to what happened to the piece of land across from the Kennedy Road settlement which was promised to Kennedy Road by Yacob Baig while campaigning for the 2000 local government elections.
- We demand an immediate investigation into the rampant corruption in the drawing up of housing lists.
- We demand an immediate investigation into the activities of the notorious Pinetown gangster landlord Ricky Govender.
- We demand an immediate investigation into the activities of the notorious police officer Glen Nayager.
- We also want to use this platform to, with our comrades who are here today from around the Province, make the following demands to the other Municipalities and to the Provincial Government:
  - The Slum Elimination Act is immoral and illegal. Our settlements are communities to be developed not slums to be 'eliminated'. This Act must be scrapped immediately.
  - There must be immediate action to prevent farm workers from being evicted, harassed and banned from visiting their ancestors' graves.
  - There must be immediate action to prevent the enclosure of land for private game reserves.
  - There must be immediate action to prevent the threatened evictions in eNkwalini
  - There must be immediate action to prevent the eThekwini & Msunduzi Municipalities as well as private landowners from continuing to carry out illegal demolitions and evictions and forced relocations to rural ghettoes like Park Gate and France.

- Those of us living in municipal flats note that in addition to providing substandard housing, the councils charge rents way in excess of our ability to pay. We therefore demand the writing-off of all rental arrears.
- We opposed the hosting of the 2010 World Cup on the grounds that we couldn't afford to be building stadiums when millions have no houses. But now that it is coming there must be an immediate commitment to declare that the World Cup will be a '100% Evictions Free World Cup' all across the province. i.e. That there will not be any evictions of shack dwellers or street traders.

Today people from around the city and the province are uniting in support of our struggle. Today we express our support for our comrades elsewhere. We stand with our comrades in Joe Slovo in Cape Town and we stand with our comrades in Protea South, Kliptown, Thembelihle, and Thembisa in Johannesburg. We also stand with our comrades in Harare, Istanbul and Port-au-Prince. We assert, in particular, our support for Shamita Naidoo, Louisa Motha and all of the people of Motala Heights who are facing violence, death threats and the constant threat of illegal evictions at the hands of Ricky Govender.

Today, we demand answers. We have approached the municipality on many occasions, and many promises have been made to us. Yet still we have no land. We still have no houses. We are still being pushed out of the cities. We still have no electricity and so we are still terrorised by shack fires. The municipality says it will house us. We demand to know when. We demand to know where. We demand to know how many houses. We demand to know who will be resettled. We demand to receive all of this information in clear language and on a regular basis and to be consulted about these decisions.

We are here to stay. We will not go away. We will not be silent.

3. Statement on the Xenophobic Attacks in Johannesburg

On 11 May 2008, xenophobic attacks began in Alexandra, Johannesburg, and quickly spread across the country. On 20 May Zodwa Nsibande returned home to the Kennedy Road settlement from central Durban and reported that she had heard people saying that attacks were imminent in Durban. The movement held a long and careful discussion to formulate its position that day and met again the following day to review the first draft of a press statement expressing the conclusions of that discussion. This press statement was very widely circulated and translated.

Wednesday, 21 May 2008
Abahlali baseMjondolo Press Statement
Unyawo Alunampumulo

Abahlali baseMjondolo Statement on the Xenophobic Attacks in Johannesburg

There is only one human race.

Our struggle and every real struggle is to put the human being at the centre of society, starting with the worst off.

An action can be illegal. A person cannot be illegal. A person is a person wherever they may find themselves.

If you live in a settlement you are from that settlement and you are a neighbour and a comrade in that settlement.

We condemn the attacks, the beatings, rape and murder, in Johannesburg on people born in other countries. We will fight left and right to ensure that this does not happen here in KwaZulu-Natal.

We have been warning for years that the anger of the poor can go in many directions. That warning, like our warnings about the rats and the fires and the lack of toilets, the human dumping grounds called relocation sites, the new concentration camps called transit camps and corrupt, cruel, violent and racist police, has gone unheeded.

Let us be clear. Neither poverty nor oppression justify one poor person turning on another. A poor man who turns on his wife or a poor family that turn on their neighbours must be opposed, stopped and brought to justice. But the reason why this happens in Alex and not Sandton is because people in Alex are suffering and scared for the future of their lives. They are living under the kind of stress that can damage a person. The perpetrators of these attacks must be held responsible but the people who have crowded the poor onto tiny bits of land, threatened their hold on that land with evictions and forced removals, treated them all like criminals, exploited them, repressed their struggles, pushed up the price of food and built too few houses, that are too small and too far away and then corruptly sold them must also be held responsible.

There are other truths that also need to be faced up to.

We need to be clear that the Department of Home Affairs does not treat refugees or migrants as human beings. Our members who were born in other countries tell us terrible stories about very long queues that lead only to more queues and then to disrespect, cruelty and corruption. They tell us terrible stories about police who demand bribes, tear up their papers, steal their money and send them to Lindela – a place that is even worse than a transit camp. A place that is not fit for a human being. We know that you can even be sent to Lindela if you were born in South Africa but you look 'too dark' to the police or you come from Giyani and so you don't know the word for elbow in isiZulu.

We need to be clear that in every relocation all the people without ID books are left homeless. This affects some people born in South Africa, but it mostly affects people born in other countries.

We need to be clear that many politicians, and the police and the media, talk about 'illegal immigrants' as if they are all criminals. We know the damage that this does and the pain that this causes. We are also spoken about as if we are all criminals when in fact we suffer the most from crime because we have no gates or guards to protect our homes.

We need to be clear about the role of the South African government and South African companies in other countries. We need to be clear about NEPAD. We all know what Anglo-American is doing in the Congo and what our government is doing in Zimbabwe. They must also be held responsible.

We all know that South Africans were welcomed in Zimbabwe and in Zambia, even as far away as England, when they were fleeing the oppression of apartheid. In our own movement we have people who were in exile. We must welcome those who are fleeing oppression now. This obligation is doubled by the fact that our government and big companies here are supporting oppression in other countries.

People say that people born in other countries are selling mandrax. Oppose mandrax and its sellers but don't lie to yourself and say that people born in South African do not also sell mandrax or that our police do not take money from mandrax sellers. Fight for a police service that serves the people. *Don't turn your suffering neighbours into enemies.*

People say that people born in other countries are amagundane (rats, meaning scabs). Oppose amagundane but don't lie to yourself and say that people born in South Africa are not also amagundane. People also say that people born in other countries are willing to work for very little money bringing everyone's wages down. But we know that people are desperate and struggling to survive everywhere. Fight for strong unions that cover all sectors, even informal work. *Don't turn your suffering neighbours into enemies.*

People say that people born in other countries don't stand up to struggle and always run away from the police. Oppose cowardice but don't lie to yourself and say that people born in South Africa are not also cowards. Don't lie to yourself and pretend that it is the same for someone born here and someone not born here to stand up to the corrupt, violent and racist police. Fight for ID books for your neighbours so that we can all stand together for the rights of the poor. *Don't turn your suffering neighbours into enemies.*

People say that people born in other countries are getting houses by corruption. Oppose corruption but don't lie to yourself and say that people born in South Africa are not also buying houses from the councillors and officials in the housing department. Fight against corruption. *Don't turn your suffering neighbours into enemies.*

People say that people born in other countries are more successful in love because they don't have to send money home to rural areas. Oppose a poverty so bad that it even strangles love. Live for a life outside of money by fighting for an income for everyone. *Don't turn your suffering neighbours into enemies.*

People say that there are too many sellers on the streets and that the ones from outside must go. We need to ask ourselves why only a few companies can own so many big shops, why the police harass and steal from street traders and why the traders are being driven out of the cities. The poor man cutting hair and the poor woman selling fruit are not our enemies. *Don't turn your suffering neighbours into enemies.*

We all know that if this thing is not stopped a war against the Mozambicans will become a war against all the amaShangaan. A war against the Zimbabweans will become a war against the amaShona that will become a war against the amaVenda. Then people will be asking why the amaXhosa are in Durban, why the Chinese and Pakistanis are here. If this thing is not stopped what will happen to a place like Clare Estate where the people are amaXhosa, amaMpondo, amaZulu and abeSuthu; Indian and African; Muslim, Hindu and Christian; born in South Africa, Mozambique, Zimbabwe, Malawi, Pakistan, Namibia, the Congo and India?

Yesterday we heard that this thing started in Warwick and in the City centre. We heard that traders had their goods stolen and that people were being checked for their complexion, a man from Ntuzuma was stopped and assaulted for being 'too black'. Tensions are high in the City centre. Last night people were running in the streets in Umbilo looking for 'amakwerkwere'. People in the tall flats were shouting down to them saying 'There are Congolese here, come up!" This thing has started in Durban. We don't know what will happen tonight.

We will do everything that we can to make sure that it goes no further and that it does not come to the settlements. We have already decided on the following actions:

1. We will resuscitate our relations with the street traders' organisations and meet to discuss this thing with them and stay in day-to-day contact with them.

2. We have made contact with refugee organisations and will stay in day-to-day contact with them. We will invite them to all our meetings and events.

3. We have made contact with senior police officers who we can trust, who are not corrupt and who wish to serve the people. They have given us their cell numbers and have promised to work with us to stop this thing immediately if it starts in Durban. We will ask all our people to watch for this thing and if it happens we'll be able to contact the police that we can trust immediately. They have promised to come straight away.

4. We will put this threat on the agenda of all our meetings and events.

5. We will discuss this in every branch and in every settlement in our movement.

6. We will discuss this with our allied movements like the Western Cape Anti-Eviction Campaign and the Landless People's Movement so that we can develop a national strategy.

7. In the coming days our members are travelling to the Northern Cape, the North West, Johannesburg and Cape Town to meet shack dwellers struggling against forced removal, corruption and lack of services. In each of these meetings we will discuss this issue.

8. We are asking all radio stations to make space for us and others to discuss this issue.

9. In the past we have not put our members born in other countries to the front because we were scared that the police would send them to Lindela. From now on we will put our members born in other countries in the front, but not with their full names because we still cannot trust all the police.

10. If the need arises here we will ask all our members to defend and shelter their comrades from other countries.

We hear that the political analysts are saying that the poor must be educated about xenophobia. Always the solution is to 'educate the poor'. When we get cholera we must be educated about washing our hands when in fact we need clear water. When we get burnt we must be educated about fire when in fact we need electricity. This is just a way of blaming the poor for our suffering. We want land and housing in the cities, we want to go to university, we want water and electricity – we don't want to be educated to be good at surviving poverty on our own. The solution is not to educate the poor about xenophobia. The solution is to give the poor what they need to survive so that it becomes easier to be welcoming and generous. The solution is to stop the xenophobia at all levels of our society. Arrest the poor man who has become a murderer. But also arrest the corrupt policeman and the corrupt officials in Home Affairs. Close down Lindela and apologise for the suffering it has caused. Give papers to all the people sheltering in the police stations in Johannesburg.

It is time to ask serious questions about why it is that money and rich people can move freely around the world while everywhere the poor must confront razor wire, corrupt and violent police, queues and relocation or deportation. In South Africa some of us are moved out of the cities to rural human dumping grounds called relocation sites while others are moved all the way out of the country. Some of us are taken to transit camps and some of us are taken to Lindela. The destinations might be different, but it is the same kind of oppression. Let us all educate ourselves on these questions so that we can all take action.

We want, with humility, to suggest that the people in Jo'burg move beyond making statements condemning these attacks. We suggest, with humility, that now that we are in this terrible crisis we need a living solidarity, a solidarity in action. It is time for each community and family to take in the refugees from this violence. They cannot be left in the police stations where they risk deportation. It is time for the church leaders and the political leaders and the trade union leaders to be with and live with the comrades born in other countries every day until this danger passes. Here in Durban our comrades stand with us when the Land Invasions Unit comes to evict us or the police come to beat us. Even the priests are beaten. Now we must all stand with our comrades when their neighbours come to attack them. If this happens in the settlements here in Durban this is what we must do and what we will do.

We make the following demands to the government of South Africa:

1. Close down Lindela today. Set the people free.
2. Announce, today, that there will be papers for every person sheltering in your police stations.
3. Ban the sale of land in the cities until all the people are housed.
4. Stop all evictions and forced removals immediately.
5. Do not build one more golf course estate until everyone has a house.
6. Support the people of Zimbabwe, not an oppressive government that destroys the homes of the poor and uses rape and torture to control opposition.
7. Arrest all corrupt people working in the police and Home Affairs.
8. Announce, today, a summit between all refugee organisations and the police and Home Affairs to plan how they can be changed radically so that they begin to serve all the people living in South Africa.

5. Organising in the Shadow of Death

This press statement was issued on 7 July 2018 in a period of acute repression and a moment of intense danger. It set out the violence, assassinations, threats and slander faced by Abahlali baseMjondolo, warned of credible plans to assassinate S'bu Zikode, and located these attacks within the wider politics of corruption and ethnic mobilisation in Durban. It was widely circulated.

Saturday, 7 July 2018
Abahlali baseMjondolo Press Statement
Organising in the Shadow of Death

Since our movement was first formed in 2005 various factions of the elite – including in the ruling party, the government,

NGOs and the universities – have considered the self-organisation of impoverished people in a democratic movement to be an illegitimate development.

All positions in our movement are subject to election, and the right to recall. We continually hold open and public meetings at which decisions are reached, usually by the process of continuing discussion until a consensus is developed. Yet despite this our decision to organise ourselves, and to speak and act for ourselves, has constantly been presented as an external conspiracy by elites who feel that they have a natural right to think for us, to speak for us and to represent us. We have regularly been presented as criminals.

We have faced constant lies and slander, some of it organised by intelligence, and serious and often violent repression including assault, the destruction of our homes, arrests and imprisonment on false charges while awaiting trial, torture and death. Our members have died at the hands of the police, the Anti-Land Invasion Unit and the izinkabi. At times some of our leaders have had to go underground and in late 2009 the whole movement had to organise underground for some months.

In 2009 our members were openly attacked by the ANC, acting with the support of the police, and driven from their homes in the Kennedy Road settlement in Clare Estate. For months our members were openly driven from their homes by armed supporters of the ruling party acting with the open support of the police. Leading figures in the ruling party publicly supported this repression.

In March 2013, Thembinkosi Qumbela, who was not a member of our movement but did support a land occupation that our members also supported, was assassinated in Cato Crest. In June the same year Nkululeko Gwala, our Chairperson in Cato Crest, was also assassinated. In September that year Nqobile

Nzuza was murdered by a police officer during a protest in Cato Crest. She was 17 years old. After a long struggle the police officer that murdered her was convicted of murder.

In September 2014 Thuli Ndlovu, our chairperson in Kwa-Ndengezi, was murdered by two ANC Ward Councillors. After another long struggle the two Councillors were convicted of murder and are now serving their sentence.

In June last year we lost two weeks old baby Jayden Khoza after he inhaled teargas when police attacked the community in Foreman Road in Clare Estate. In the same month Samuel Hloele was murdered by the Anti-Land Invasion Unit in what was then eMasenseni and is now the eKukhanyeni land occupation in Marianhill. In November our chairperson in the Sisonke Village land occupation in Lamontville, Sibonelo Mpeku, was kidnapped and murdered.

On 17 December 2017 Soyiso Nkqayini and Smanga Mkhize, were shot by unknown men in the eNkanini land occupation in Cato Manor. Comrade Smanga was seriously injured and Comrade Soyiso, the Youth League organiser in the occupation, passed away. In January this year Sandile Biyela, was killed while escaping a brutal police attack on the Solomon Mahlangu land occupation near Chesterville. On 22 May S'fiso Ngcobo, our chairperson in eKukhanyeni, was assassinated. On 29 May S'bu Zikode suddenly lost control of the car that he was travelling in. When the car was taken to a mechanic it was found that it had been deliberately tampered with. This was a clear attempt on his life.

Qumbelo, Gwala, Ndlovu and Ngcobo all knew that they had been marked for death before they were assassinated. Today we are hearing the same things that we heard before their murders. We have the same sense that we had before their murders, a sense that death is imminent.

As we have previously noted the Mayor and the Chief Whip in the eThekwini Municipality made disturbingly undemocratic, authoritarian and threatening statements about our movement, and about S'bu Zikode, at an Executive Committee on Tuesday, 12 June 2018. The Mayor, Zandile Gumede, said that there was a 'third hand' behind our movement. She also said that the City would not work with our movement and would, instead, work with the South African Shack Dwellers' International Alliance – the South African branch of the international NGO that used to be known as Shack Dwellers International (SDI). The Chief Whip, Nelly Nyanisa, said that S'bu Zikode is "hellbent on making the city ungovernable". She also issued a clear threat against our movement saying "We will deal with them." This was all reported in the media. Similar statements were made by ANC leaders prior to the attack on our movement in Kennedy Road in 2009.

Since these statements were made by the Mayor and the Chief Whip we have had numerous warnings from various credible sources that S'bu Zikode's life is in grave danger. These warnings have come from people in the ANC and people in the police who are opposed to the political gangsterism in Durban. Some members of the police in Durban have often been directly supportive of, and involved in, political gangsterism and repression. But there are factions in the police, especially at national level, that are opposed to this. We have and will continue to work with them to achieve credible investigations into the murders of our comrades, and the plan to assassinate S'bu Zikode, with the aim of achieving arrests and prosecutions. At the same time we will continue to build democratic people's power from below and in struggle.

We have been warned from credible sources that the ANC in Durban is planning to present our movement as a 'terrorist' organisation to legitimate further repression. We have been through this kind of experience before when we have been presented as criminals, and as a 'third force', to justify repression. We repeat that we are a democratic organisation, with an audited membership in good standing of more than 50,000, that takes its important decisions in open public meetings. We stand for justice, and the dignity of our members.

The courts have repeatedly found in our favour and have repeatedly noted illegal conduct against our members by the eThekwini Municipality. Our aspirations for land, housing and dignity are firmly in accordance with the spirit of the Constitution of the Republic.

Our members freely participate in the formation of the movement's positions, sometimes over many months of discussions in numerous meetings. This includes any collective decision that we may take about a strategic response to elections. In this regard, as in all other matters, our leaders follow the mandate generated in free and open discussion by our members. Our leaders do not give a line to the members. This is a fundamental part of our politics.

There are two main reasons why we are facing such extreme hostility from the ANC in Durban. One is that the Zuma faction has had to retreat to the City of Durban, and the City's large budget. This faction is organised around corruption and the housing budget is one of the most important vehicles through which corruption is organised. We oppose corruption, often very effectively, in communities across the city. The Zuma faction is also trying to build an ethnic project. Our movement unites people from various ethnicities, races and nationalities in a democratic struggle for justice. This also makes us a direct threat to the Zuma project. We have held public assemblies of up to six or seven thousand people in football grounds. This is far more people than Zuma can get at his court appearances, even with a huge budget.

We will not retreat. We have faced and survived previous waves of repression, especially in 2009, and again in 2013 and 2014. We have faced and survived all kinds of dirty tricks and lies. In 2018 we are bigger and stronger than we have ever been before. We will survive this wave of repression too.

However, we wish to make it clear that if another attempt is made on S'bu Zikode's life, or on the life of any one of our members or comrades, we will hold Zandile Gumede and the eThekwini ANC directly responsible.

We are calling for national and international solidarity with our movement and in defence of democracy in Durban.

The politic of blood in this city and province must come to an end. We will not rest until justice has been served for every one of our members and comrades who have been murdered. Every assassination of every person, without regard for the organisation in which they held membership, must be thoroughly investigated with a view to achieving a successful prosecution and conviction.

We stand for peace and justice.

6. Memorandum on the Decommodification of Access to Land

On Monday 24 February 2020 thousands of comrades marched on the Durban City Hall to present the movement's position on the land question in response to the ANC's move to legislate for 'expropriation without compensation'. The movement's position emerged through careful discussion in many meetings, held at all levels of the movement, over several months.

24 February 2020

Constitutionalise the Right to Land!

We, members and supporters of Abahlali baseMjondolo Movement SA, street traders, hostel dwellers and workers in South Africa are democrats committed to the flourishing of this country.

We speak for ourselves and direct our own struggle. We have no hidden agenda. We have been mobilised by our own suffering and our hopes for a better future. It is time to take seriously that access to land is a serious problem in our country, that land was stolen from our ancestors and continues to be allocated and managed in the interests of elites and private profit, and that all this has impoverished us, and continues to impoverish us. It is time to take seriously that housing in Durban is a mess that has not just terrorised our communities but made us homeless. It is time to take seriously that raising questions about land and housing has led to us being murdered with impunity. In municipalities like eThekwini we have been murdered in broad daylight.

Abahlali has, since its formation in 2005, called for the right to well-located land and decent housing for all in our cities. In our first legal march in 2005 we called for the expropriation of land from below. We specifically targeted Moreland, the largest private land owner in Durban which had close links to the then Mayor, Obed Mlaba.

From the beginning our movement rejected the idea that land should be turned into a commodity, something to be bought and sold. We insisted that land should be distributed on the basis of human need and we affirmed the need for grassroots urban planning, and for the bottom up and democratic management of land. We insisted that women must be full and equal participants in all decisions relating to the allocation and management of land. However, the state was prepared to put the commercial value of land before its social value. Profit was put before human needs. Lies were put before the truth. When there was land reform it was captured by the elite. Our suffering became a way for people in the ruling party to become rich.

It is not just that the state has failed to provide land for us. The state has also tried to violently remove us from the bits of land that we have been living on. Our movement has had to struggle against violent and unlawful evictions in our cities. We have resisted against the Red Ants of the City of Johannesburg. We have resisted against the Land Invasion Unit of the City of Durban and, yes, we have resisted against the Law Enforcement of the City of Cape Town. Many of us have terrible scars. Some of us have lost our lives in these struggles. We have been lied to, arrested, beaten, tortured in police custody, assaulted, and slandered in the media.

As a result of the state and the ruling party using violence to prevent us from accessing land we have had to undertake a programme of land reform from below. We have organised numerous successful land occupations. At the moment we have more than seventy branches on active land occupations. When we have insisted that the social value of land must come before its commercial value this has not just been empty words. We have made this a reality, through struggle. Our movement has paid a very high price for standing firm for the position that land, wealth and power should be shared. Many of our comrades have lost their lives in the struggle for land, and it is a fact that cannot be denied that for impoverished black people the price for land continues to be paid in blood. In our meetings it is common to hear people saying "umhlaba noma ukufa".

The inequality, impoverishment and unemployment that we face today are as a result of the failure of the state to return land to the people. It is a disgrace that the black majority government has, over twenty-five years in power, failed to redress the oppression of the past and to break with the capitalist system for distributing and managing land. The collapse of the economy today cannot be avoided unless the state takes a radical shift towards a fair distribution of all kinds of wealth, power and opportunity in the economy, including land. This is also urgent in the rural areas. The inequalities and poverty that exist in rural

South Africa today will continue for as long as the land remains in the hands of the white commercial farmers and those traditional leaders that are corrupt and authoritarian. They will continue for as long as some traditional leaders are corrupt and bought by the rich, including mining companies, at the expense of the communities. They will continue for as long as the government's limited land reform programme continues to be captured by the elites.

Our movement has had series of careful discussions, involving large numbers of people, about the Constitution and the Eighteenth Amendment Bill, Expropriation of Land without Compensation. The Ad hoc Committee on the Amendment of Section 25 of the Constitution of the Republic of South Africa, 1996 has been mandated with this task and has called on all South Africans to submit their proposals.

We agree to the 'expropriation of land without compensation' proposal. However, we do not agree that land must be taken from white elites and be given to black elites. This will have not make a fundamental change to the deep inequalities and oppression that exist in this country. We cannot trust the ANC, or any of the political parties in parliament, to ensure that land is distributed to the people on a fair and democratic basis. There is no party in parliament that represents the interests of the impoverished, that refuses corruption, that is committed to revolutionary democracy and is willing to be led from below.

Abahlali's position is that land should be seen as a public good and not as private property and as a commodity. Land should be made a 'right' and not a form of property. We also do not agree that the state must own the land on behalf of the people because the state itself in its current form cannot be trusted. Land must be distributed to the people, and managed, on a democratic basis, from below.

Eighteen of our comrades have been killed as a direct result of their participation for the struggles to insist that land must be shared on an equal basis amongst those who live on it or work it. Those who claim to be custodians of our laws have been implicated in the murders of our comrades. Two ANC councillors have been found guilty of the murder of one of our leaders by a court of law and are serving life imprisonment. This is another reason why we want our communities to have direct and collective ownership of land, and to be able to manage land through their own democratic structures.

Abahlali is well aware that laws on paper often mean little or nothing for people in reality. We understand that laws can change for the better and that the oppressed can remain oppressed. For this reason, while we oppose bad laws, like the Slums Act, and support good laws, we remain highly aware that oppression can only be effectively opposed when the oppressed are organised to build their own democratic power from below. Building our own democratic power is the most important way for us to advance our struggle.

However, Abahlali supports the motion to Amend Section 25 of the Constitution of the Republic of South Africa 1996. Section 25 in its current form has been one of the drivers behind the inequalities, impoverishment and unemployment that has terrorised this country. However, this support is not in any way to agree with what many politicians and parties are proposing. The preamble should explicitly make land a 'right' to be enjoyed by all and not property that may be bought and sold. We note, also, that Section 26 of the Constitution guarantees the right to Housing however, that right becomes impossible without the right to land. These proposals must apply to all land both in urban and rural areas, and to residential, agriculture and commercial land.

For too long the right of women to land has been denied for many reasons. We call on the full realisation of the right of all women to access and manage land, just like their male counter parts, and without any conditions imposed. We oppose all forces that use the language of culture to justify patriarchy and we oppose all forms of patriarchy, wherever we encounter them.

Furthermore, if a new law is passed it must also make all evictions illegal, commit the state to supporting land occupations with the development of infrastructure and abolish all the armed units set up in the big cities to attack land occupations.

Abahlali has resolved that we will engage in a mass action to have our position and our submission clear, clean and loud instead of making an online submission by one technical individual. Our members have demanded that they want to be involved in this strategic submission given that land is their life and, too often, their death. We have resolved that today, 24 February, a few days before the closing date for submissions, we march here in our numbers to collectively submit our proposals. We have asked for the Chairperson of the Ad hoc Committee on the Amendment of Section 25, Dr Mathole Motshekga to come and receive our submission.

We know that there is a long road ahead of us and that we need to intensify our political strategies through ongoing organisation, discussion and mobilisation, including rolling mass action. Today's action takes place in Durban, but we continue to work to build popular democratic power in other provinces where we have branches, including the Eastern Cape, Mpumalanga and Gauteng.

We are also aware that this struggle will not end here today, or in parliament, but in people's day to day struggles and realities. This may mean that, Section 25 or no Section 25, the "people shall govern".

7. S'bu Zikode's Remarks to the UN Committee on Economic, Social and Cultural Rights

30 September 2020

Opening remarks by S'bu Zikode at the 68th Session of the UN Committee on Economic, Social and Cultural Rights

S'bu Zikode

Thank you, Mr. Chairperson, members of the ESCR-Net and the Committee for the ESCR for affording us with such an important platform to express our concerns.

Across the world, residents of the shack settlements, many of which are in fact land occupations, are not recognized as human beings who can think for themselves. We are not treated with respect and dignity, or taken seriously. We are treated as if we are beneath the law. The state often engages us with violence rather than discussion. Some NGOs and some media have presented us to the world as criminals. For too long we have been living in substandard housing conditions, with no access to water and sanitation. For too long we have been denied access to roads.

We have been denied refuse collection and electricity provision. The failure to provide electricity has caused regular shack fires in shack settlements resulting in the loss of many lives. We live, year after year, like pigs in the mud in the summer when it rains, and with fire after fire in the winter.

When state assisted housing and job opportunities are provided they are allocated along party lines. In the case of South Africa, if you are not connected to people in power you do not get a job or house in our shanty towns. If you stand up to this you will be at a very high risk of violence.

For too long local politicians have become dangerous figures in our communities in the name of leadership, law and order. Our movement has lost 18 activists who have been murdered. Some have been murdered by local politicians of the ruling African National Congress, some have been murdered by the state and its police. Some have been murdered by municipality's land invasion units and by private security companies. Recently we have been subject to sustained violence from Calvin and Family Security Company. Across the world, activists are targeted and attacked for demanding social justice and decent living conditions.

For too long our efforts to organize the oppressed and build the democratic power of the oppressed has been met with state violence. Organizing outside the state and the ruling party has been criminalized. If we take democracy seriously we are met with violence.

We have been denied access to well-located urban land where we can be closer to areas of active economic opportunities, we can have access to health care facilities and our children can have access to better education. Globally, states are prioritizing economic and political interests over basic human needs.

We are implementing a programme of land reform from below with organized land occupations. But this is a difficult and dangerous politic. Grassroots urban planning is not recognized by the state and they use all forms of violence to try and crush it.

What we need is for the allocation of land to be removed from state and capitalist control and to be organized on a democratic basis. There should be a total decommodification of land. Land was not bought and sold before colonialism and it should not be bought and sold now.

For too long brutal and illegal evictions have been terrorizing communities, even during a pandemic that requires us to stay at home for public health reasons. We therefore demand an end to all evictions in our cities. We demand an end to all land dispossession, utilities cut offs and related attacks on the poor.

The politicians continue to try and divide the oppressed by turning neighbour against neighbour with xenophobia and other forms of prejudice and discrimination. All progressive movements must do all that they can to oppose this. The strength of the oppressed lies in our unity.

State corruption is a great threat to future stability in our countries. We demand an end to all state corruption that has robbed our communities of the right to access all economic, social and cultural rights as enshrined in the international laws and standards.

Land, wealth and power must be shared equally. The right to housing and a life lived in dignity must be guaranteed for all. We call this a living communism, a politic in which every person counts as a person, the dignity of every human is respected, there are no more human borders and the brutal centuries during which colonialism and capitalism have drenched the world in blood are finally brought to an end.

8. S'bu Zikode's Per Anger Prize Speech

S'bu Zikode was awarded the 2021 Per Anger Prize which is awarded annually by the Swedish government for courageous commitment to human rights and democracy. This is the speech that he gave at the awards ceremony.

21 April 2021

Per Anger Prize Speech

S'bu Zikode

The price for land, for decent housing and the right to the city is paid in blood. Brutal and unlawful evictions continue to terrorize our communities.

No human being should live in substandard housing conditions, without access to basic services such as water and sanitation, where there is no road access, where there is no electricity and where there is no refuse collection.

I have dedicated my life to the fight for equal rights for all South Africans. And I am deeply honoured and humbled to stand here today, and receive the Per Anger Prize – a prize named after a man who bravely resisted fascism, and saved many lives.

I want to extend my deep gratitude to the jury, the Living History Forum, Minister Amanda Lind and Afrikagrupperna for nominating me.

We all know that many of the people of Sweden, as well as their government, gave strong support to our people during apartheid. So, it is an honour to receive a prize like this from the Swedish government.

I have been carried through the last fifteen years by the movement Abahlali baseMjondolo, a movement of the poor, of people living in shacks. We have more than 80,000 members, the majority are women. Membership and leadership are open to all without regard to ethnicity or national origin.

We insist that the dignity of all human beings must be recognised. We should be included in all decision making that affects us, our right to the city should be recognised, our settlements should receive adequate services and we should be able to build our homes and communities in peace.

We wish to see a much deeper form of democracy in our country, and in the world.

We resist the idea that because we are poor, we must be confined to the dark corners.

We have organised in solidarity with struggles all over the world, and built relationships with movements in different countries. The struggle is global.

The award of the Per Anger Prize means that our struggle for land, decent housing and dignity has been recognised as just and legitimate in Sweden. It is an acknowledgement that the poor have experiences and ideas from which others can learn. They can learn from the courage of the Abahlali members who have continued to organise despite repeated violent evictions, serious intimidation, and assassinations.

An award for me is also an award for the movement, and for the determination and courage of all the people who have kept our movement going for fifteen years, despite very serious repression which has included arrests, death threats and murders.

Per Anger was a brave man. Our comrades who have lost their lives – people like Thuli Ndlovu, Nkululeko Gwala and others – were brave people. Today courage meets courage. Principle meets principle.

No legitimate and democratic movement, or activist, should be criminalized and attacked when organising to build the power of the oppressed from below. All evictions leading to homelessness must be stopped and those responsible for illegal and violent evictions must face criminal charges.

The poor are not poor by choice. It is the history of colonialism, apartheid and land dispossession that keep us in deep poverty. The commodification of land and state corruption keep us poor. This is why the social value of land must come before its commercial value. This is why it is important to organise, to build democratic power from below. This requires building solidarity between and within struggling communities. This is what has kept us strong.

It is very dangerous to be an activist in South Africa, and in many countries around the world, because we are well organized and can stand firm to protect our rights. This is perceived as threatening to people in power.

There is a serious problem of political gangsterism in South Africa, and especially in the city of Durban and the province of KwaZulu-Natal. Hundreds of people have been assassinated.

Corrupted politicians who enrich themselves and their families at the expense of millions of poor people of South Africa have often objected our work. They have used the police, militarized private security guards and izinkabi (hitmen) to kill us.

Abahlali have faced serious repression. We have been beaten, tortured in police custody, slandered in the media and subject to open death threats. Some of us have been murdered with impunity.

I am among those who have suffered serious repression – including arrest, torture, the destruction of my home, slander, and death threats.

In a period of ten years our movement lost eighteen activists. The price for land and dignity has been paid in blood. These murders have not been investigated. Our lives count for nothing to the state and to much of society. We are treated as if we are beneath the law. This award says that our lives count to you. This kind of support forces the repressive forces that we confront to recognise that we are not people that do not count. It helps to keep us safe.

Today I call on the people of South Africa, mostly young people as they are the future of our country and the world, to support our struggle for land, decent housing and dignity. I also call on the government of South Africa to stop evicting poor people and to stop the use of violence when dealing with poor people. I call on the government to consider putting the social value of land before its commercial value. I also call on the government of South Africa to protect and uphold our hard-won constitutional democracy.

You have my deep gratitude, and the deep gratitude of Abahlali baseMjondolo. I hope that we can work together to continue the struggle to humanize the world.

Together, we stand for dignity, respect and democracy.

We are all people that count.

Thank you!

9. The Blood of the Palestinians is our Blood

The movement is deeply committed to internationalist positions and understands the struggle to humanise the world to be a global struggle. It affirms solidarity with all oppressed people everywhere. Solidarity with Palestine has been central to its internationalist commitments since the beginning.

12 May 2021
Abahlali baseMjondolo press statement
The Blood of the Palestinians is our Blood

Our struggle is rooted in the principle that the recognition of our full and equal humanity is non-negotiable. We also insist that this principle is applied to all people everywhere. There can be no group of people whose humanity is denied.

As everyone knows a shared experience of colonial dispossession and oppression – and of apartheid – means that most South Africans have a deep understanding and concern for the suffering and struggle of the Palestinian people.

As poor black people in South Africa today our homes continue to be violently destroyed, we continue to be governed with armed force, often militarised force, and we continue to be attacked with state violence, arrested on trumped up charges and assassinated. Our humanity is constantly denied and our dignity is constantly vandalised.

Because of our past and our present we have a deep sense of solidarity for the Palestinian people who continue to suffer under an extremely brutal colonial occupation. Their pain is our pain. We know what it means to live not knowing whether your home and that of your children will be destroyed. We know what it means to live without the protection of the law, and under a state that considers you outside of the law. We know what it means to have innocent people in jail, people whose only crime was to stand up for justice.

The Israeli state is a criminal state, guilty of a long crime against humanity. Its system of apartheid, and the everyday violence and brutality with which it is enforced, must be condemned by all in the world. It is racism that leads many of the powerful countries in the world to be quiet when Israel continues to oppress and murder the Palestinians. It is the same racism that leads some of the world's media to refuse to accept that what is happening in Palestine is a matter of brutal colonial oppression and not 'clashes' or an issue of 'disputed' neighbourhoods and land.

Many people have lost their lives in the current attacks. These attacks are motivated by hatred and a deliberate attempt to undermine the dignity of people.

Those who support the attacks on the Palestinian people, or who remain are silent as they witness repression, are as guilty of the atrocities as the government of Israel. Zionism became politically dominant through war and remains dominant because of the global system of imperialism. In 2019 the government of the United States US provided $3.8 billion to the Israeli military. One settler colonial state supports another. African-Americans are shot on the streets by the police and migrants are treated like criminals in the United States while in Palestine people suffer extreme day to day oppression and have their homes stolen and destroyed, their sacred places vandalised and their people murdered.

The world must be humanised.

We stand with the people of Palestine. We will work with all other progressive organisations to support the work to build solidarity with Palestine in South Africa and elsewhere. Any Palestinian activist who is in South Africa and wishes to meet with us will be treated as an honoured guest in our occupations.

10. KwaZulu-Natal and Gauteng are Burning: We Need to Build a Just Peace

This statement, prepared through a careful process of consultation with all the branches in the affected areas challenged the dominant understanding of the early period of the riots, and became a major national intervention.

Tuesday, 13 July 2021
Abahlali baseMjondolo
KwaZulu-Natal and Gauteng are burning, we need to build a just peace

Abahlali baseMjondolo has always warned that the anger of the poor can go in many directions. We have warned again and again that we are sitting on a ticking time bomb.

We have warned for too long that people cannot continue to live in terrible poverty only to be ignored year after year. We have made it clear that people will not allow their humanity to be vandalised forever. For too long we have been explaining that we are ruled with violence and that the public often accept this by their silence.

The state has brought us violence each time we protest peacefully. When we deliver a memorandum, it will be thrown in the bin. Each time we engage the authorities in good faith only to be lied to and deceived. Each time when some sort of services or jobs are provided they are only given to members of the ruling party.

Our homes have been repeatedly destroyed with violence, in some cases more than 30 times. Municipalities like eThekwini have been ignoring court orders. Shack dwellers have been treated as if we are beneath the law. In all this, lies are put before the truth, promises made are broken, profit is put before people's needs and the commercial value of land continues to be put before its social value.

The riots that have been happening have nothing to do with Zuma. Poverty and hunger were a bomb and the break down in order caused by Zuma's people lit the fuse. Everywhere people who started taking food from the shops said that they are starving and have nothing to do with Zuma and are not doing anything for him. Migrants were also taking food. Everyone who lives in South Africa was taking food because the issue was hunger and poverty.

Many people were hungry before Covid. Now they have been starving since March last year. Many lost jobs and those few who were getting the R350 grant which was making a difference to their lives have lost it. More than 74% of the youth are unemployed.

The elites have always ignored the poor. They do not see us. When the riots happened suddenly the poor were before their eyes.

But the poor will remain poor after the riots. In fact, our lives will probably be much worse. If you ask people what they will eat after the riots are finished they say that they are hungry now. They will say that hunger is more deadly than Covid. If you ask them about the people who will lose their jobs they say what about our children who graduated but have no jobs? People are only looking at the present, and not the future. This is because they do not feel that they have a future.

Many people are afraid that there will be no more food to buy and that when all the food taken in the riots is finished an even bigger hunger is coming. People are worried that unemployment will get worse. Others are afraid that there will be fires in the shacks because some people are drinking so much looted alcohol. Many Zimbabweans are saying that this reminds them of how the collapse started in Zimbabwe and now that things are so bad it is better for them to go home.

Hunger has turned some people into evil hearts in such a way that they can no longer even consider another person. Tavern owners are angry that they are still paying rent for their shops but they are closed while restaurants are open. There are people who are pushing the agenda of the Zuma faction in the chaos. People are saying that it was ordinary hungry people who took the food, but that it is Zuma's people who are burning the factories, warehouses, malls and infrastructure. What will happen to people's jobs now that factories and other places of work are being burnt? That is not a revolution. It is destruction that will leave the poor poorer.

In the beginning all kinds of poor people were taking food. Now under the surface the xenophobic and ethnic murmurs are starting. Xenophobia and tribalism are coming. Some people are worried that there will be a tribalistic war between Africans and Indians. Local ANC structures are encouraging divisions, often using social media.

It cannot be normal to have more than 42% of the country's population unemployed. It cannot be normal to have such a high level of state corruption. It cannot be normal to have the poor ruled with so much violence from the state and the ruling party.

In October 2020 our movement took to the streets with nearly 5,000 people in protest against state corruption. We marched against violent and unlawful evictions that have become normal in our communities, and of course we marched against violence on minority groups and women. Nobody took us seriously. Even today the office of the Premier of KwaZulu-Natal pretended as if he was doing something about it only to create the fatal ground for what we see today.

The government is useless. Zuma and Ramaphosa both failed the poor. The government has failed to bring food and peace. The state teaches the people violence and not discussion and negotiation. Corruption continues. People are very angry about Zweli Mkhize who was stealing from us while we were not able to work and going to sleep hungry. Sihle Zikalala has not come out clearly to say what needs to be said by a real leader. He is a big part of the problem. People were very angry after the President's speech on Monday. He said nothing about the R350 grant, unemployment or hunger. He said nothing about the fact that even our educated children sit at home and do nothing, or that we no longer have money to send our children to school because all the money that we can find must be used to buy food. He said nothing about the fact that the politicians and their families have been eating while we starve.

We fear that the economic situation will become like Zimbabwe, and that when the worms have finished eating the carcass they will eat each other.

The country is a mess and there is lack of leadership. On the first day it was young people taking food. Now it is old people too. Ramaphosa should understand that when mothers and fathers are going out to loot the situation in the country is hopeless and that the government has failed. He should understand that while there has been criminality the riots were the result of starvation. We need food, we need money and we need to be left alone on our land but instead Ramaphosa is sending us soldiers. Deploying the army is very risky as it could escalate the situation which could mean more death. Government cannot just address people through the television screens and think everything will be ok. People who say that they are leaders should be on the ground, with the people, in this crisis.

It is high time that the ANC takes responsibility for this crisis. The level of arrogance that we have witnessed in the past needs to come to an end. It is time that they swallow their pride if they really care about this beautiful country. They need to able to put the people of South Africa first unlike Zandile Gumede who told the media that the ANC comes before South Africans.

We note that when an ANC faction instructs people to loot there are no police, no helicopters and no water cannons. But when we have a peaceful rally or a march, or build a home, there are all kinds of police resources in place.

The situation is tense and our members are very worried. A process of carefully listening towards the feelings and views of our members has shown that they say that for too long, they have been ignored as if they do not exist in this country. They say that for too long they have lived without employment and in deep poverty. They say that they have not had food for their families while politicians loot the state and enrich themselves. They say that the Covid-19 lock down hit us very hard but the state has stopped the Covid-19 grant despite taking the country back to alert level 4.

Our position, based on these listenings, is as follows:

Zuma and Ramaphosa have both failed the poor.

The riots are a result of starvation and not support for Zuma.

We remain committed to the Constitution because the law gives us some protection from the political gangsters in the ANC. Without the law repression would be much worse. We would just be ruled by violence. Therefore, the Constitution must be defended at all costs.

The Covid grant needs to be immediately reinstated and increased and all unemployed people must get a grant. Nobody can be without an income.

Food parcels need to be made available in all communities. They need to be given directly to hungry people and not to councillors who are mostly corrupt and in support of Zuma.

There must be a rapid release of land for housing and community farming and an end to evictions.

Urban farming cooperatives must be supported with seeds, fertilizer, tools and land.

There needs to be a serious programme of job creation.

If Zikalala can't come out with a clear statement in support of the people he must be removed from office. He needs to immediately call for calm in the province, provide clear leadership and assure the safety of the people. All he does is give statistics of the fatalities and the extent of damage.

We all need to call for calm and peace, and to work for calm and peace.

All forms of xenophobia and tribalism must be opposed.

There need to be dialogues in each city and province, and nationally, on how to build peace and justice. This must include all membership-based grassroots formations to pave the way towards an inclusive future for South Africa. These dialogues can begin the process of forming solidarity councils in each city.

We repeat that people are not interested in Zuma's arrest. It is the fact that they have been unemployed and hungry for too long that has created this crisis.

Our movement has been very clear in all our actions and popular education that ubuhlalism and the living politic are central to the course of our struggle. We spend so much of time educating our members about ubuntu and that umuntu ungumuntu ngabantu. With these teachings and emphasis, we want to reflect the kind of society we are advocating for. This is the most important part of the work we do before we actually engage on our living conditions and struggles for land, housing and dignity. Here we argue that unless we are responsible human beings with love their country and fellow humanity, we will not win the battle of justice and equality.

In the past we have stood victorious against many forms of violence organised by reckless politicians through xenophobia and ethnicity. We have built strong values of ubuntu and maintain high discipline in the mist of these challenges of state violence, poverty, unemployment and inequality.

Our members say that if Abahlali baseMjondolo was in charge we would be swimming together in the red sea.

Ungovernability will leave us poorer and more divided. The government of the ANC has failed. We need a new form of democratic government, a government of the people organised from below, to rebuild our society.

We will do all we can to bring peace, and to build a just peace. Join us or work with us as we work towards a world in which each person counts as a person, a world in which the dignity of every human being is respected.

11. UnFreedom Day to be Marked in Three Provinces

In 2023 the movement was, for the first time, able to hold UnFreedom events in three provinces. The statement issued in advance of the events draws together different threads of Abahlali's struggle over the years – against assassination, repression, corruption and dispossession – into a comprehensive indictment of a democracy captured by elites and hostile to the poor.

25 April 2023
Abahlali baseMjondolo press statement
UnFreedom Day to be Marked in Three Provinces

Impoverished people are not free, and when the ANC and the government lie to us and tell us that we are free they insult our intelligence and our humanity.

We are not free because we are assassinated and murdered by the izinkabi and the police.

We are not free because our homes are attacked and destroyed by the state.

We are not free because we are denied the right to well-located urban land and thereby our right to a place in the cities.

We are not free because we are forced into government shacks (so called 'transit camps') and left to rot there.

We are not free because our attempts to build autonomous and democratic communities in which access to land and housing is decommodified are repressed with violence from the state and the ruling party, including murder.

We are not free because the food system remains in the hands of capital and our struggle to build food sovereignty from below is met with a denial of access to land and violent repression, including murder.

We are not free because a whole range of elite forces, including the ruling party, the state and some NGOs and academics do not accept our right to think, decide and act for ourselves.

We are not free because the economic system that makes some people to be rich and other people to be poor continues to destroy our lives, and leave millions of us to suffer the fear, pain and indignity of poverty.

We are not free because the demand for radical democracy – for a bottom up system based on worker and community control – made by the trade unions and community organisations in the 1980s was denied.

We are not free because the state is an instrument for capital and the political class to exploit and repress us rather than an instrument of the people to build a just society.

We are not free because people born in other countries live under constant pressure and in constant fear.

We are not free because women are not respected and safe.

We are not free because LGBTQI+ people are not respected and safe.

We are not free because society is becoming more and more violent.

We are not free because we live in a society that denies our humanity and vandalises our dignity every day, year after year.

We will not be free until land, wealth and power are shared fairly, every person has the right to organise freely and safely and to participate in all decision making that affects them and the humanity and dignity of every person is respected.

Our movement has marked UnFreedom Day since 2006. In the beginning the ANC tried to ban UnFreedom Day and sent out police in armoured vehicles and a helicopter to try and suppress our right to gather in rejection of fake freedom.

Seventeen years later we still live under a fake freedom. Last year four of our comrades were murdered, one by masked police officers and the other three by the izinkabi, while a number of our leaders were jailed on fake charges.

Today the worsening economic crisis, exacerbated by the electricity crisis, is crushing our lives and our hopes. Most young people are without work and most families can't afford to eat healthy food. Many people are going hungry. It is a very painful thing for any parent to put their child to bed on an empty stomach. The ANC has such contempt for us that even in this crisis it is failing to provide nutrition for schools in KwaZulu-Natal.

This economic crisis hits the poor and marginalised the hardest. Our government does not have the political will to solve the issues that the country is facing. It is a government of capital and corruption, not the people. Grants must be defended and extended but a life on grants is not a full life. Land and wealth must be fairly shared among the people, among all the people.

The wealth controlled and regulated by the state was not built by the politicians. It is not their private property. The wealth of the few comes from the dispossession and exploitation of the many. We were made poor so that others could be made rich and we are kept poor so that others can remain rich. The wealth of society belongs to the people. It is public wealth.

Public funds must be used for the public good. Corruption is theft from the public, theft that hits and hurts the poor the hardest. Corruption is always an attack on the people. It always robs our communities of the potential to improve our living conditions and to thrive.

Society is becoming more and more violent and politically connected mafias are taking over more and more institutions and communities. Corruption is the order of the day. The state has become an instrument of accumulation rather than an instrument of the people. We are not safe. We are ruled by violence.

The state does not treat us like other people. We are regularly ignored, insulted, harassed, assaulted and robbed by state officials. The state regularly destroys our homes and our street stalls at gunpoint. Some of our neighbours and comrades have been murdered by the state. Across the country the state regularly abuses and murders poor black people. Bheki Cele has made no effort to deal with the assassinations of our members and must be removed from office with immediate effect.

The councillor system has not only become a system of top-down political control. Many councillors see their position as nothing but an opportunity to grow rich from public funds, from the wealth of the people. Some councillors are a danger to our democracy and our communities. In some wards people are terrorised by the councillors and their committees.

This democracy was not won by the politicians, and it does not belong to them. It was won by the struggles of the people including organisations like the ICU, Fosatu, the UDF, Cosatu and others, organisations with members who were poor and working-class people like us. This democracy belongs to the people, and we are part of the people. Today democracy is defended by the courage and struggles of the people, people like us, and people like Babita Deokoran, Tebogo Mkhonza, Nokuthula Mabaso, Thuli Ndlovu and many, many others who have given their lives in the struggle against fake freedom.

The counter-revolution against the struggles of the people by the ANC has to be faced. The ANC cannot 'self-correct'. Its twenty-nine years of rule have been a disaster for the poor. Incredibly the poor are now both greater in number and poorer than in 1994 while the rich have been getting richer and richer. The ANC has no concern for the people and it cannot be trusted. In fact, the ANC is now the enemy of the people.

We are left to live in shacks, including so called government 'transit camps'. We are left to burn in the shacks and to be murdered in the shacks. We are left to die alone. We are in very difficult times. We have no one but ourselves.

Under these circumstances it would be highly irresponsible to accept the lie that we are now free, that the ANC brought freedom to us and that we should obediently celebrate our freedom.

The decision to mark UnFreedom Day 2023 was taken in open general assemblies, in free and public discussions. Events will be held in three provinces. The schedule of events is as follows:

KwaZulu-Natal: On 26 April there will be a march in Durban from Curries Fountain to the City Hall.

Mpumalanga: On 28 April there will be a march from Vukuzakhe Location to the Volksrust townhall.

Gauteng: On 29 April there will be a rally in the Good Hope Settlement in Germiston.

All events are scheduled to start at 9 am.

Land. Dignity. Freedom.

Organise, mobilise and build towards a movement of communes!

12. The People's Minimum Demands

Beginning at the General Assembly held in Durban on the first Sunday in February 2024 the movement held an extensive process of meetings and discussions at all levels of our movement, and in all the 87 branches in good standing across the four provinces where the movement had members, to develop a collective strategy for the election to be held on 29 May 2024. The Youth League and Women's League also held their own discussions. The discussions in our monthly General Assemblies were all open to the public and were attended by representatives from several other organisations. A three-day camp for leaders from all provinces was held from 22 to 24 March in the Valley of a Thousand Hills. At this camp the discussions that had been taking place since early February were synthesised into a list of demands that were then presented at a General Assembly on 7 April where they were discussed and adopted.

The People's Minimum Demands

1. Well located urban land must be made available for people to be able to build homes and other community infrastructure, including community gardens. This will require a land audit to make planning effective.

2. Those who wish to receive government housing and meet a reasonable income criteria should be placed on the housing list. Government housing must be built at scale and with urgency and must be decent and fit for human beings. Transit camps must be rejected as an insult to the dignity of the people. The housing list must be transparent and neither renters nor any other particular group of residents should be excluded from the list.

3. There must be a serious commitment to affirming and defending the dignity of the people, of all the people including the poor and all vulnerable groups.

4. There must be a clear and viable plan to provide either decent jobs or a liveable income for all. While youth unemployment is a particularly severe crisis, people over 35 must be included in this plan. Informal forms of work should be respected, supported and, where there is danger and exploitation, regulated to ensure safety and fair labour practices. This must include sex work.

5. There must be an end to the criminalisation of land occupations which need to be understood as a form of grassroots urban planning. When there are genuine social complications around land use these must be resolved with negotiation and not with state violence.

6. Existing shack settlements and new occupations must receive collective tenure and the provision of non-commodified access to basic services such as water, electricity, sanitation and road access, and refuse collection must be undertaken as an urgent priority.

7. There should be extensive state support for community gardens including seeds, tools, irrigation and fencing, as well as participatory workshops in agroecological farming methods. The state should also support a system of community-controlled markets for produce to be sold. People receiving grants from the state should be able to use their cards to buy at these markets.

8. There must be a clear and viable plan to end load shedding that includes commitments to provision for access by the poor, to a responsible transition to socially owned and managed renewable energy and to ensure that workers in the current system are not discarded.

9. There must be lifelong, free and decolonised education available to all, irrespective of age. Education must include skills for people to be able to find employment and develop their communities as well as forms of education that are simply there for people to develop themselves. Community run creches and schools (along the lines of the Frantz Fanon School in eKhenana) should receive state support if they meet clearly elaborated criteria for democratic management and a social function.

10. There must be state support for democratically run communes and cooperatives and the tendering system should, wherever possible, transition from supporting private business towards supporting cooperatives.

11. There needs to be a clear plan to address the crisis in the health care system, which must include employing many more doctors, nurses and other health care workers. The overcrowding of clinics and hospitals must be addressed.

12. There needs to be a clear plan to address the crisis of violence in society, including violence against women, as well as other forms of socially damaging behaviour. This must not take the form of escalating the endemic state violence against the poor but should rather take the form of building a more peaceful, safe and just society.

13. There needs to be a program to decentralise access to educational opportunities and possibilities for employment to ensure national access, including in rural areas.

14. Political parties need to have a clear program to develop the intellectual strength and integrity of their leaders, and to do the same for government officials.

15. Corruption needs to be understood as theft from the people and to be dealt with decisively. After due process any politician shown to be guilty of corruption must be suspended

from their political party for a period of five years, after which rehabilitation can be considered if there is genuine acknowledgment of wrong doing. Any official seeking to extract bribes, to sell houses or to only allocate houses, services or any other benefits to members of a particular political party must be swiftly investigated and, after due process overseen by an elected jury from the affected community, dismissed from their position.

16. There must be a serious commitment to dealing with the environmental crisis from a people centred perspective. This includes effective action to stop the dumping of rubbish in shack settlements.

17. Participatory democracy – affirmed under the slogan 'nothing for us without us' – must be committed to as a clear principle to guide all engagements between the state and the people. This is particularly important at the community level.

18. There must be clear opposition to the genocide being carried out in Gaza, and a clear commitment to freedom and justice for the Palestinian people, and for all oppressed people everywhere.

19. There must be a clear rejection of xenophobia, ethnic politics, sexism, discrimination against LGBQTI+ people and all other attempts to divide and weaken the people.

20. There must be a clear commitment to oppose all forms of political violence and political repression in South Africa, no matter which person or organisation is suffering political violence or repression. This commitment cannot be limited to empty words and must be backed up with real action including mass mobilisation, media campaigns, legal action, etc. There must be a commitment to work against political violence and repression with all political forces opposed to political violence and repression.

13. Thapelo Mohapi's 'Everybody Thinks!' Speech

This speech was presented to the conference of the Development Studies Association by Thapelo Mohapi on 28 June 2024 on a panel organised by the Translocal Learning Network.

Everybody Thinks!

When our movement started in 2005 many of the people who founded the movement insisted that everybody thinks, and that the poor must be given the same right as everyone else to participate in all discussions and decision making affecting their lives and communities, as well as wider issues.

There were two reasons for this. One was that the ruling party and the government thought that its role was to think for poor people. The second was that some NGOs and academics also thought that their role was to think for poor people. This included liberals and the kind of leftists who see their role as giving political direction to the oppressed rather than working with the oppressed on the basis of mutual respect.

It is important to understand that colonialism did not just expropriate land and cattle from African people, and then labour. It also expropriated the right of African people to make decisions about their own lives and communities. Just as we struggle for land to be returned to the people, and to be shared fairly among the people, and just as we struggle for wealth to be restored to the people, and to be shared fairly among the people, we also struggle for the right of all people to be able to participate in all discussions and decision making.

This is why we adopted the slogan 'Nothing for us without us!' which was originally developed by the disabled movement in the United Kingdom. This is why we adopted the phrase 'grassroots urban planning' from our comrades in the urban movement in Brazil. This is why Ashraf Cassiem, the leader of the militant

Western Cape Anti-Eviction Campaign developed the slogan 'We are poor not stupid!'.

We insist that the poor must be afforded the opportunity to be part of their own development whether this is autonomous self-organised development from below or development that emerges from engagement between the oppressed and the state and NGOs.

It is often perceived that when you are poor and living in shack settlements, former Bantustans or on white farms, you cannot think about how the future development of your community must take shape. This is often the perception of the Western donors who fund governments and NGOs in Africa. This is seen as a 'realistic' view and the idea that poor people can think and plan for ourselves is dismissed as 'romantic'.

Such thinking leads to development being imposed on communities, sometimes at gun point. Sometimes some people in communities, a small minority, are paid to support the development against the majority who do not support this. This divides communities and leads to tensions and revolts in communities. Sometimes what is called 'development' is actually just more oppression, such as when people are forcibly removed from centrally located shack settlements to human dumping grounds far from the cities, dumping grounds where there are no opportunities for people. All this could be avoided if poor people were taken seriously as people, as people with the same right to participate in discussions and decisions as all other people. Being poor does not mean that your capacity to think for yourself has collapsed. Every human being can think. Being poor means that you don't have money, not that you don't have a mind.

Many communities who have occupied land in our movement have planned their development without the interference of government and NGOs in the community. Autonomy, self-organisation and self-management have achieved some incredible results, radical results.

One example is the eKhenana land occupation in Durban which was developed into a commune. There you can see the results of careful, collaborative grassroots urban planning with well laid out homes as well as a communal garden, a communal poultry project, as well as a Political School that is named after the great revolutionary intellectual Frantz Fanon. A high price was paid for this. Three comrades were assassinated.

No government or NGO official would understand the need to centre development around a political school. This is because the poor are seen as victims who need services to be 'delivered' not as political protagonists who want to change the world from below. For us building communes means building the political power of the poor from below as well as meeting basic material needs.

Not long ago the municipality tried to evict Hlanganani (meaning 'coming together'), one of our occupations in Salt Rock, on the north coast of KwaZulu-Natal. The people in the community resisted the eviction and forced the municipality to listen to them. They refused to be treated as human waste and protested to demand their recognition as human beings. This led to the municipality in KwaDukuza to finally recognising them as people and giving them the dignity that they deserve. Respectful engagement is usually something that must be struggled for.

Today the community are part of the development in their community. They discuss and plan as a community on how the area can be developed. This has made the work of the municipal officials much easier. The development will not only provide housing, it will also provide skills that will create employment opportunities beyond the development. This happens because the community is part of the development.

We have made real progress with both completely autonomous forms of development and forms of development with the state, but in both cases progress is only possible when people insist on the right to think and decide for themselves. In both cases people had to be organised and had to resist the forces of repression before progress could be made.

Often when people refuse to be treated as people who can't think and have no right to think the first response of the state (or NGOs, academics, etc) is to claim that someone is else is thinking for them, remoting them from behind, and to criminalise the community or its leaders.

We don't need think tanks to think for us. We don't need people who have never lived in a shack settlement to think for us. We need people who are willing to think with us. For university educated people this requires that they are willing to humble themselves, to understand that they are people among other people. People can learn important skills in universities but these skills need to be brought into conversation with the people, with the organic thinking of the people.

A radical state, NGO or academic should understand the difference between charity provided to victims of history and solidarity with people who are committed to making history, to changing the world. Development should be about popular political empowerment as well as meeting basic material needs.

Everybody thinks!

14. Building peace and unity in a traumatised community

This statement was issued after serious divisions emerged in eKhenana. It describes the incredible trauma caused by relentless repression and conflict and how this led to internal divisions. It affirms the principles of the movement and sets out a path to rebuild unity and democratic life.

21 November 2024
Abahlali baseMjondolo press statement
Building peace and unity in a traumatised community
Ukwakha ukuthula nobunye phakathi kwabalimele

Our movement currently has over 150,000 members organised into 93 branches in four provinces. The process to join the movement and form a branch in good standing is slow and careful, and the requirements for a branch to sustain membership of the movement include rigorous adherence to the principles of the movement, including a clearly specified set of democratic practices. To ensure that branches remain committed to the principles of the movement, including democratic practices and organisation, membership must be periodically renewed and new elections held.

There have been cases where the affiliation of branches to the movement has lapsed due to a failure to elect new leaders for various reasons, including the emergence of serious divisions in a community. There have also been cases where a branch has had to be suspended until it can resolve problems that have arisen. When the membership of a branch has lapsed or been suspended and we are asked to assist in working to resolve problems and restoring its affiliation to the movement, we always provide support. When divisions have emerged we always try to work towards healing and building unity.

There have also been cases where we have had to recall members from positions of leadership for conduct that violates our principles. In 2014, we had to expel a person in a senior leadership position due to serious corruption that had devastating consequences for a whole community. In 2018 some leaders were recalled from their positions after agreeing to take money from VBS bank in exchange for offering political support to the Zuma faction of the ANC. When there is acknowledgment of wrongdoing on the part of individuals, we also work towards healing.

We have all been damaged by oppression, and we all continue to be damaged by oppression, and so our politics must be grounded in the work of collective healing. We all come out of a history of serious violence from colonialism, to apartheid, the civil war in KwaZulu-Natal, and ongoing violence and repression, and so our politics must be grounded in the work of building peace. We have been committed to this work of healing and building peace for almost twenty years.

Branches often face serious challenges in the struggle to hold land, to ensure that land is not commodified, to sustain democratic practices and to sustain the progress required to develop occupations into communes. Many branches have faced repeated state violence, evictions, attempts to take over land and occupations by local party thugs, arrests, imprisonment and killings whether by the izinkabi, the police or municipal or private security. Recently, both the Sihlalangenkani Commune in Salt Rock on the North Coast of KwaZulu-Natal and the Lindokuhle Mnguni Occupation on the East Rand in Gauteng have faced militarised 'raids' from combined forces drawn from private and state security.

Repression always results in trauma and anxiety and can sometimes result in paranoia and serious divisions in movements. People who have suffered serious repression can come to feel that they should have a special standing in a movement, a standing above democratic processes. This, like the risk of paranoia and division, is common to all movements facing serious repression and is something that must be handled with great care and sensitivity.

In recent years, the eKhenana branch in Durban has faced the most severe repression suffered by any of our branches, including numerous violent attacks from the state and the imprisonment and assassinations of activists.

The struggle for land in eKhenana has suffered serious repression by the municipality, a notoriously violent ANC ward councillor and local ANC thugs trying to make money from land and housing. Because the initial occupation was chaotic and unplanned there was not a clear and shared sense of how it should be organised. There were disputes between people who wanted to sell and rent land and shacks and those who wanted to build a commune in which land and shacks are not rented and sold. This created a complex situation with multiple pressures. The severe violence and repression that people have suffered has resulted in terrible trauma, including among the children who have seen and lived with things that no child should ever see or have to live with.

As we explained in a statement issued on 10 May 2021, "the eKhenana Occupation has not been an easy occupation and the road to its current achievements was very difficult." The land was occupied in August 2018 and the eKhenana branch was first launched on 14 April 2019. However, serious division and conflict emerged in the branch, and there were credible allegations of abusive behaviour by some individuals. As a result the branch's membership of our movement was suspended in September 2019. As we explained in the statement issued at the time, "As a result of the failure of the branch to address these issues swiftly and effectively, it was shut down and the membership of all the residents was terminated. The residents were advised to organise an assembly open to all to discuss the issues, to work to resolve the issues, and then work towards relaunching the branch."

The work to resolve the problems was begun and on 5 October 2020, an election was held and the branch was relaunched as an affiliate of our movement. The branch suffered extreme repression, including three assassinations, in 2022. One of our members was murdered by a masked police officer in the nearby eNkanini branch in the same year.

The branch was scheduled to renew its membership and hold a new election on 1 October 2023. However, they were not able to go ahead with the election and the renewal of the branch membership as serious divisions had emerged within the branch. After a discussion, we agreed that the branch would hold its election and have its membership renewed on 30 November. However, the leadership of eKhenana cancelled the scheduled election and membership renewal set for 30 November. We were expecting them to propose a new date, but they did not.

As is standard in our movement, they had a three-month grace period to hold the election and renew their membership during which they could continue to participate in the movement with all rights and responsibilities. However, they did not set a new date, and so their membership automatically lapsed after three months, which was 1 January 2024. As a result of this we have not had any members in eKhenana since the beginning of this year. The community has not elected a new structure and, therefore, does not currently have an elected leadership. In a situation like this where there is no elected structure the only way to avoid factionalism and engage openly and fairly is via well attended community assemblies open to all residents.

Our movement has never recruited members. People come to the movement if they wish to join, after which a process has to be followed to build democratic structures before a branch can be launched. It can take months or even years for a branch to achieve full membership. We also do not try and persuade branches to sustain their membership. The same principle applies – branches must choose to join the movement and to remain in the movement. Of course, if people request our support to work towards launching or renewing the membership of a branch, we gladly provide that support. If we do not receive such a request we do not intervene and, of course, we cannot speak or act for a community or faction of a community who are not members of our movement.

In September this year, we were approached by a group of residents from eKhenana who explained that serious divisions and problems had emerged in the community. They said that they wanted the help of the movement to work towards resolving these problems, building unity and moving towards the reestablishment of a democratic branch council and a renewal of the affiliation of the branch to the movement.

As a result, meetings were held with eKhenana residents on 10, 26 and 29 September 2024 and again on 18 October. In these meetings it became clear that there were serious tensions between a small group of residents and the rest of the community, and between that same small group of residents and former residents of eKhenana who had fled during the violence and now wish to return. The people who wish to return are former members of our movement whose legal right to be present on the land was confirmed in a court judgment won against the municipality. It has been said that they are ANC members trying to take over the land but this is not true.

It became clear that there are a few people who, as often happens under conditions of severe repression, have started to see everyone else as the enemy, including former comrades on the land and former comrades who wish to return to the land. Serious complaints were made about a small group of residents. Serious complaints had previously been made about two of these residents. In such circumstances, it is always our responsibility to listen to everyone and to listen very carefully.

It was agreed to hold an open public meeting, open to all residents of eKhenana across the divisions that had emerged, on Sunday 10 November with the aim of building peace and unity.

The meeting was opened by S'bu Zikode, whose first words were "We are here to bring peace, unity and stability". Zikode went on to recognise and honour each and every life that has been lost in eKhenana. There was also an opening prayer for peace from Pastor Errol Khumalo.

The meeting was very well attended. A total of 54 residents attended the meeting, 36 women and 18 men, which, in this now very small community, means that almost all residents were present. After careful discussion, the majority of the residents committed to a process of building peace and unity, and 48 people signed a declaration committing to this. However, six people in the minority faction in the community did not sign the declaration.

With a clear majority of the residents in support of the process to build peace and unity we have agreed to proceed with the process, a process grounded in healing. We will continue to make it clear to the six people who did not want to commit to the process that they are welcome to join the process at any time. If this process goes well, eKhenana will be able to elect a new council with a mandate to represent the community. If that council wishes to relaunch the eKhenana branch and take membership of our movement, it will be warmly welcomed back into the movement. If it wishes to be independent we will gladly work in solidarity with them when asked to do so as we do with many other organisations such as the Congolese Solidarity Campaign, the South Durban Community Environmental Alliance, Ubunye bamaHostela, etc, etc.

There are some challenges. The breakdown in the relationship between a small group of people and the rest of the community as well as former residents who wish to return to the land is serious. There are credible allegations of unacceptable behaviour. There is paranoia and there has been serious dishonesty. However, when there is enough commitment, healing can happen, and unity rebuilt in difficult circumstances. We have recently achieved a successful healing process with the former leaders of our movement who were recalled from their positions in 2018. We are hopeful that we can do the same in eKhenana despite the severity of the trauma that people have suffered and the seriousness of the divisions in the community.

We have agreed to start the process of healing, which will include ceremonies and prayers of all religions at eKhenana. Traditional healers will also participate. We are also asking progressive social workers and psychologists to volunteer to work with traumatised residents. Healing will be a process, and the residents will require all possible forms of ongoing support.

The work of struggle is the work of healing, and the work of healing is the work of struggle.

15. Solidarity with SERI and Other Organisations Under Attack by Operation Dudula

On 17 July Abahlali baseMjondolo confronted, outnumbered and humiliated Operation Dudula in Braamfontein in Johannesburg. It was the first time that this violent fascist organisation had been confronted by the left. This is the statement that was issued on the morning of the confrontation.

17 July 2025
Abahlali baseMjondolo Press Statement
Solidarity with SERI and Other Organisations Under Attack by Operation Dudula

Around the world, right-wing forces are scapegoating migrants for the devastation caused by capitalism and, in countries like South Africa, extreme corruption.

Our movement has always put human dignity at the centre of our struggle. We began our struggle by demanding the recognition of our own humanity and dignity from the ANC and the state which were vandalising our humanity.

We do not only struggle for the recognition of our own humanity. Every human being, everywhere, must be counted as a human being. We are in solidarity with all oppressed people everywhere. We are in solidarity with the people of Palestine, Swaziland and the Congo. We are in solidarity with the young people facing the police on the streets of Nairobi, with people resisting ICE in the United States, and with everyone who resists the vandalisation of humanity.

In 2008, when the first wave of serious xenophobic violence began in South Africa, we held an urgent discussion and issued a strong and clear statement of our principles. We noted that we had been warning for years that the anger of the poor can go in many directions, and we affirmed the principle that a person is a person wherever they find themselves: Unyawo alunampumulo. We agreed that we would shelter and defend people under attack.

That statement can be read here: https://abahlali.org/node/3582/

We have held to these principles and have worked closely with migrant organisations, worked to support migrants to organise themselves, and welcomed everyone into our movement and into its leadership. Wherever we organise, we make it very clear that opposition to xenophobia is a fundamental principle of our movement.

In recent weeks, Operation Dudula – which has a long history of violent attacks on migrants – has been blockading the entrances to public hospitals and aggressively denying people they claim are not South African access to healthcare. This is an all-out and cowardly attack on vulnerable people. It is a deep shame on our country that there are groups openly and violently denying other human beings the right to access healthcare simply because they were born in another country.

Our public healthcare system is in crisis as a result of many years of austerity, which has seen budgets ruthlessly cut year after year; mismanagement by political appointees; and massive looting by politically connected operators, some of them operating as violent mafias.

Scapegoating migrants for this crisis, and aggressively denying them access to hospitals, is not just cowardly and cruel – it is also a form of public political miseducation that diverts attention away from the real causes of the crisis.

Today, Operation Dudula will march on the Socio-Economic Rights Institute (SERI) and other organisations, accusing them of being 'unpatriotic' for including migrants in the legal support that they offer to all people in South Africa whose rights are under attack.

SERI has represented a number of organisations, including our movement, in court action against Operation Dudula for assaulting, intimidating and generally harassing and abusing migrants. Details of the case against Operation Dudula can be found here: http://bit.ly/4gwnjNO

If 'patriotism' is misunderstood as dehumanising and scapegoating some of us who live in this country we want nothing to do with it. However, the patriotism with its roots in the vision of a just society that was developed in the struggle against apartheid, the struggle in which the South African nation was built, is a patriotism that we can and do support. We love our country and we struggle with and for all oppressed people to build a better South Africa for all of us who live here.

When we heard that Operation Dudula was going to march on SERI and other organisations we discussed this at our General Assembly in Durban. Our members decided that we should meet with Operation Dudula. They decided that the meeting should begin by acknowledging that South Africans are and should be angry at massive unemployment and impoverishment, collapsing services and institutions and very high rates of violence.

Our members thought that once we had agreed on this we should discuss the real reasons for the suffering of the people, and the need to affirm and defend the humanity of all people.

We contacted Operation Dudula to request a meeting but they refused to meet us, saying that we are also 'unpatriotic' and that we have taken them to court.

Our movement has a long history of support from SERI. They are genuine movement lawyers who have worked with respectful, principled and dedicated commitment year after year. Working in partnership with SERI we have won many victories for our members. Some of these victories have benefited poor people as a whole. SERI are our comrades, and we will stand with them, as we stand with all people and organisations under attack from Operation Dudula, or any other expression of fascist politics.

Today we will be on the streets, outside the SERI office, in solidarity with our comrades and in defence of our principles. Just as we cannot allow the vandalisation of the humanity of others, we cannot allow our own humanity to be disgraced.

These are trying times in our country that require all of us to work together to build the unity of the oppressed and to build powerful movements for justice. We must direct our anger where it belongs – at the state, the government, the ANC and the capitalist system – and not at people who were born in other countries.

We must not allow right-wing forces to justify violence against the people in the name of the people. The political forces that try to divide the oppressed – to turn people against their neighbours – are always the enemies of the oppressed, and the struggle for justice.

If Operation Dudula change their minds we remain willing to meet them in order to discuss how to understand the real causes and nature of the crisis that we all face and to unite the poor and the working class to build a peaceful and just society.

Abahlali baseMjondolo Chronology

2004

National "rebellion of the poor" with widespread protests. S'bu Zikode resigns from the ANC.

KRDC declares 2005 the "Year of Action" after promised housing land sold for brick factory.

2005

16 February: Mass meeting at Kennedy Road resolves to blockade Umgeni Road if promises ignored.

19 March: Kennedy Road blockade of N2; 14 arrested, many beaten.

21 March: 1,200 march on Sydenham Police Station; attacked by police; detainees spend 10 days in custody.

13 May: 3,000 march on Councillor Yacoob Baig demanding land, housing, resignation.

14 September: 5,000 march again on Baig; mock funeral staged; protesters attacked by police and arrests made.

4 October: 1,000 Quarry Road residents march on Councillor Jayraj Bachu; mock funeral staged.

4 October (later that day): 14 settlements meet at Kennedy Road; Abahlali baseMjondolo founded.

21 October: Mhlengi Khumalo (1 year old) dies following a shack fire in Kennedy Road; memorial held 28 October.

9 November: S'bu Zikode writes *We Are the Third Force*, published in the *Daily News* and widely republished.

14 November: The March on Mlaba organised from Foreman Road is illegally banned, police attack and people are injured and arrested.

10 December: Abahlali participates in the Social Movements Indaba in Johannesburg.

2006

The movement begins to expand into Pinetown from its original base in Clare Estate, Sydenham and Reservoir Hills.

12 February: Abahlali is denied entrance into the Cato Crest Hall after being invited to a live SABC Asikhulume recording.

27 February: An interdict is granted against Mike Sutcliffe preventing him from banning Abahlali marches.

1 March: The movement boycotts the local government election under the slogan 'No land! No House! No Vote!"

21 April: KwaZulu-Natal announces the Slums Bill (Elimination and Prevention of Re-emergence of Slums Bill).

27 April: First UnFreedom Day.

1 September: Provincial ANC leaders try to ban AbM from speaking to the media.

12 September: S'bu Zikode and Philani Zungu arrested, assaulted, and tortured.

December: AbM, AEC and LPM protest at the SMI meeting at the Centre for Civil Society.

2007

March: Kennedy 6 arrested on false charges, hunger strike.

10 April: March on Glen Nayager at the Sydenham Police Station in protest at police brutality and harassment.

27 April: Second UnFreedom Day march, attempted municipal ban.

24 May: Kennedy Six banning order lifted, bail granted.

29 June: KwaZulu-Natal legislature passes Slums Act.

28 September: Peaceful march to the offices of Yakoob Baig attacked in Sydenham.

2008

January: Nkosingiphile Cwera (4 months) dies after rat bite in Kennedy Road.

27 March: Charges against Kennedy 6 dropped.

21 May: Public statement opposing the xenophobic attacks; movement protects migrants and there are no attacks in any of the settlements where the movement has an organised presence.

12 June: Durban High Court grants interdicts against Ricky Govender and others after intimidation in Motala Heights.

16 June: The Youth League is formed.

8 August: The movement organises its first event in Cape Town, a workshop on the City's housing plan.

9 August: The Women's League is formed.

4 December: eMacambini residents, supported by Abahlali, blockade the N2 and R102 against the proposed AmaZulu World theme park project by Ruwaad Holdings that threatened to displace around 10,000 families.

2009

January: Abahlali challenges attempts to remove Siyanda families to the Richmond Farm Transit Camp.

26 September: Armed attack on Kennedy Road; two killed, 1,000 displaced; Zikode and others underground.

14 October: Constitutional Court strikes down Slums Act provisions.

2011

18 October: Membership reaches 10,000 people in 64 settlements.

5 November: March to demand the removal of Nigel Gumede.

2012

27 January: High Court sets aside Shallcross eviction.

19 September: Court orders permanent housing for 37 families.

25 September: AbM files damages claim over 2009 attack.

7 December: Palmiet Road march proceeds after prohibition overturned.

2013

The movement becomes active in Cato Crest, marking its expansion across Durban.

28 March: Interim interdict granted allowing the municipality to demolish and evict at will.

26 June: Nkululeko Gwala assassinated in Cato Crest.

3 July: Nkululeko Gwala's funeral held in Inchange.

21 September: ALIU shoots three AbM members.

26 September: Coordinated Road blockades.

30 September: Nqobile Nzuza (17) killed by police.

2014

6 April: Bandile Mdlalose expelled.

7 May: Tactical call to vote DA.

27 September: The movement relaunches in the Western Cape in an attempt to address the problems in its Cape Town membership.

29 September: Thuli Ndlovu assassinated; ANC councillors later convicted.

2015

Direct ties with Brazil's MST begin and the first comrade from the movement attends the Florestan Fernandes National School.

20 August: High Court sets aside 2013 interim eviction interdict.

15 October 2016: The Good Hope branch is launched in Germiston, Gauteng.

2016

6 February: Isaac Mabika killed.

18 May: Abahlali first begins to speak about a "gangster state" in its public statements.

26 August: Inkosi Thulani Mjanyelwa murdered outside his home in Dindini Village, Mbizana.

5 November 2016: S'bu Zikode meets Pope Francis during the 3rd World Meeting of Popular Movements.

2017

6 February: The movement announces that a branch-by-branch membership audit shows more than 20,000 members in good standing.

17 February: The movement launches a branch in Bizana, its first branch in the Eastern Cape.

29 May: Baby Jaydon Khoza dies from teargas at Foreman Road.

12 June: The movement launches its first branch in Mpumalanga at Vukuzakhe (Ermelo).

13 June: Samuel Hloele killed during an eviction in eKukhayeni.

19 August: The movement launches its first two branches in Gauteng.

19 November: Sibonelo Patrick Mpeku murdered in Sisonke Village, Lamontville.

17 December: Soyiso Nkqayini killed at eNkanini.

2018

10 February: The Vusimuzi branch is launched in Thembisa, Gauteng, marking an important step forward in the expansion of the movement into Gauteng.

22 May: S'fiso Ngcobo assassinated in eKukhayeni.

May-December: S'bu Zikode underground after threats.

16 September: Leadership recalled at General Assembly after corruption scandal linked to VBS.

8 October: Massive march enables S'bu Zikode to return from underground.

2019

August: The eKhenana occupation is founded in chaotic circumstances.

20 November: Melita Ngcobo, a leader in Vusimuzi in Thembisa, Gauteng, is arrested and assaulted by the police.

27 December: Court interdict halts evictions.

2020

24 February: March in Durban for total decommodification of land; call for land as public good under collective control, "umhlaba noma ukufa."

24 April: After repeated illegal evictions at eKhenana despite a court interdict is won; an Anti-Land Invasion Unit officer responds by firing live ammunition at residents.

2021

eKhenana begins to develop into a commune.

25 March: S'bu Zikode is awarded the Per Anger Prize.

21 April: The movement announces that it now has more than 80,000 members in good standing.

4 May: Mqapheli Bonono is arrested in the movement's offices in Durban on trumped up charges.

20 May: Mqapheli Bonono is granted bail and released from prison.

13 July: The movement issues a statement on the riots in KwaZulu-Natal and Gauteng, describing their first days as a mass food riot born of hunger and desperation, not support for Jacob Zuma.

4 October: All charges against Mqapheli Bonono are dropped.

2022

8 March: Ayanda Ngila is assassinated in eKhenana.

5 May: Nokuthula Mabaso is assassinated in eKhenana.

20 August: Lindokuhle Mnguni is assassinated in eKhenana.

2023

The land on which the Lindokuhle Occupation now sits is occupied over a few days in early February.

15 March: Khaya Ngubane is convicted for the murder of Ayanda Ngila.

26 April: UnFreedom Day march focuses on Palestine.

31 July: The movement announces that it has more than 120,000 members in good standing in four provinces.

2024

3 February: Process to draft People's Minimum Demands begins.

22–24 March: National leaders' camp finalises demands.

7 April: Parties (excluding ANC, MK, DA) attend Assembly to respond.

21 April: UnFreedom Day: Tactical support for EFF announced, conditional on demands.

21 November: The movement announces that it has over 150,000 members organised into 93 branches in four provinces.

2025

Membership passes 180,000 people organised into 102 branches.

19 July: After a process of healing and democratic reconstitution the eKhenana branch is relaunched with an elected council.

22 July: The movement confronts and humiliates Operation Dudula in Johannesburg.

14 September: A branch is launched in Flagstaff in the Eastern Cape marking further expansion into the province.

In Memoriam

This is a list of all the people who have lost their lives during the course of our struggle.

Mthokozisi Thabani Ndlovu

Killed on 26 September 2009 during the violence that ensued during the attack on our movement and amaMpondo people in Kennedy Road by an ANC linked mob. He was stabbed to death.

Ndumiso Thokozani Mnguni

Killed on 26 September 2009 during the violence that ensued during the attack on our movement and amaMpondo people in Kennedy Road by an ANC linked mob. He was stabbed to death.

Thembinkosi Qumbelo

Killed on 15 March 2013, following several death threats made against him. Qumbelo was shot by a group of 4 unknown men outside a tavern. Thembinkosi Qumbelo was the president of Cato Crest Residential Association.

Nkululeko Gwala

Killed on 26 June 2013 after receiving multiple threats. Gwala was shot twelve times outside his shack in Cato Crest. Nkululeko Gwala was a prominent member of Abahlali baseMjondolo.

Nqobile Nzuza

Killed on 30 September 2013 at a road blockade staged by Abahlali members in Cato Crest. Nzuza was shot twice from behind with live rounds fired by a police officer. Nqobile Nzuza was a 17-year-old girl and a supporter of Abahlali baseMjondolo.

Thuli Ndlovu

Killed on 29 September 2014. Ndlovu was shot seven times in her home. Ndlovu had been threatened for exposing corruption in KwaNdengezi. Two ANC councillors and a hitman were convicted of Ndlovu's murder. Thuli Ndlovu was the chairperson of the Abahlali baseMjondolo branch in KwaNdengezi. She was 36 years old when she was killed.

Isaac Mabika

Killed on 6 February 2016 after being attacked with an axe in Briardene by an unknown man. Mabika was a branch coordinator.

Jaydon Khoza

Killed on 29 May 2017. Baby Jaydon Khoza was two weeks old when he died after inhaling tear gas from his home in Foreman Road. Police responded to a road blockade by throwing teargas into the settlement.

Samuel Hloele

Killed on 13 June 2017. Hloele was shot to death in eKukhanyeni, Marianhill. It is alleged that his killers were members of the eThekwini Municipality's Anti-Land Invasion Unit, who were conducting evictions and firing live ammunition. Samuel Hloele was 29 years old at the time of his death.

Sibonelo Patrick Mpeku

Killed on 19 November 2017 following his kidnapping on 11 November 2017. Mpeku was a victim of numerous threats made by prominent ANC leaders. Sibonelo Mpeku was the chairperson of the Abahlali branch in Sisonke Village and he was 32 years old at the time of his death.

Soyiso Nkqayini

Killed on 17 December 2017. Nkqayini was shot by unknown men in the eNkanini occupation in Cato Manor. Soyiso Nkqayini was a vocal Youth League organiser for Abahlali baseMjondolo.

Sandile Biyela

Killed on 11 January 2018. Biyela was electrocuted when he ran into electrical wires while fleeing from police who were firing live ammunition at the protestors from the Solomon Mahlangu Abahlali baseMjondolo branch.

S'fiso Ngcobo

Killed on 22 May 2018. Ngcobo was shot to death in his home by unknown men and had been the subject of multiple death threats. S'fiso Ngcobo was the chairperson of the eKukhanyeni Abahlali baseMjondolo branch in Marianhill. He was a highly respected member of his community and is remembered for founding a crèche in eKukhanyeni and for his leadership.

Chief Thulani Mjanyelwa

Killed on 26 August 2018. He was hacked to death by a mob outside his home. Thulani Mjanyelwa was the Inkosi of Bizana in emaMpondweni in the Eastern Cape and was well known for his vocal activism in defence of land and against harmful mining practices. He was strongly supportive of our movement.

Senzo Gumede

Killed on 22 December 2018. Gumede was shot and killed by unknown gunmen after he was previously threatened by the ANC ward councillor and taxi bosses who opposed road blockades. Senzo Gumede was a prominent defender of the eKhenana occupation.

Odwa Mbana

Killed in April 2019. Mbana was shot to death after receiving several threats by local ANC members. Odwa Mbana was an Abahlali baseMjondolo Youth League organiser in eKhenana who was in his early twenties at the time of his death.

Sandile Dlamini

Killed in October 2019. He was assaulted to death by unknown men believed to be from the neighbouring area. His lifeless body was later found when the community was informed that a member of the eKhenana Abahlali branch was beaten up and lying on the ground. Sandile Dlamini was a resident of the eKhenana occupation in his mid-30s when he was killed.

Xolani Ndlovu
Killed on 1 November 2019. Ndlovu was shot to death by two unknown gunmen outside his home in eKhenana. Xolani Ndlovu was a resident of the eKhenana occupation.

Bheki Mdluli
Killed in February 2020. Mdluli died after being shot in the abdomen. He was in his late 30s at the time of his death and was known for resisting the attacks on the eKhenana occupation.

Nkosinathi Mngomezulu
Died in July 2021. In September 2013, Mngomezulu was shot while physically resisting the unlawful demolition of his shack. He was shot four times in the stomach by a security officer in the eThekwini's Anti-Land Invasion Unit. He died in 2021 from medical complications related to the injuries he sustained in the 2013 shooting. Nkosinathi Mngomezulu was a resident of the Cato Crest settlement.

Zamekile Shangase
Shot and killed outside her home in an illegal raid by the police on 29 July 2021 in Asiyindawo in the Madlala shack settlement near Lamontville. She was a branch leader of Abahlali.

Ayanda Ngila
Killed in eKhenana on 8 March 2022 after he was shot by a group of men linked to the local ANC leadership. At the time, Ngila was the deputy chairperson of the eKhenana branch. Ngila was 30 years old at the time of his death.

Siyabonga Manqele
Killed at the eNkanini Occupation on 12 March 2022. Manqele was shot in the back of the head during a raid on eNkanini during which his wife, Thandeka Sithunsa, was arrested.

Nokuthula Mabaso

Killed in eKhenana on the evening of 5 May 2022. She was shot seven times in front of her home. She was a prominent leader in the Women's League and played a central role in defending the occupation against evictions and sustaining the commune's various operations. She was also a witness to the killing of Ayanda Ngila.

Lindokuhle Mnguni

Killed in eKhenana on 20 August 2022. He was shot several times in his home after spending months in hiding. His partner, Sindiswa Ngcobo, was also shot but was fortunate to survive. Mnguni narrowly escaped harm when Ayanda Ngila was killed. Mnguni was the chairperson of Abahlali's eKhenana branch and a leader in the Youth League. He was 28 years old at the time of his death.

EU Safety Information

Publisher: Daraja Press, PO BOX 99900 BM 735 664 Wakefield, QC J0X 0C2, Canada

info@darajapress.com | https://darajapress.com

EU Authorized GPSR Representative: Easy Access System Europe – Mustamäe tee 50, 10621 Tallinn, Estonia, gpsr.requests@easproject.com

For EU product safety concerns, please contact us at info@darajapress.com